BIBLICAL ANTIDOTES

to Life's Toxins

BIBLICAL ANTIDOTES
to Life's Toxins

Glenn K. Gunderson Jr.

with Kathy Gisi Wimbish

HENDRICKSON PUBLISHERS, INC.
P.O. Box 3473
Peabody, Massachusetts 01961-3473

Text design by Kevin van der Leek Design Inc.

Bible photo: Chris Thomaidis / Stone
Prescription pad photo: Siede Preis / PhotoDisc

Printed in the United States of America

First printing—April 2003

Scripture quotations marked "NKJV" are taken from the New King James Version, copyright © 1982 Thomas Nelson, Inc. Used by permission. All rights reserved.   Scripture quotations marked "TLB" are taken from The Living Bible, copyright © 1971 Tyndale House Publishers, Wheaton, Ill. Used by permission.   Scripture quotations marked "NIV" are from the Holy Bible, New International Version, copyright © 1973, 1978, International Bible Society. Used by permission of Zondervan Bible Publishers.   Scripture quotations marked "NASB" are from the New American Standard Bible®, copyright © 1960, 1962, 1963, 1968, 1971, 1972, 1973, 1975, 1977, 1995 The Lockman Foundation. Used by permission.

Library of Congress Cataloging-in-Publication Data

Gunderson, Glenn K., 1956-
     Biblical antidotes to life's toxins / Glenn K. Gunderson, Jr. with Kathy Gisi Wimbish.
     p.   cm.
     Includes bibliographical references.
     ISBN 1-56563-799-2 (pbk.)
     1. Christian life—Baptist authors. 2. Emotions—Religious aspects—Baptists.
3. Christian life—Biblical teaching. 4. Emotions—Biblical teaching.
I. Wimbish, Kathy Gisi. II. Title.

     BV4597.3.G86 2003
     248.8'6 — dc21

                                                                        2003005423

*It is with great love and appreciation
that I dedicate this book to my wife, Kimberly,
and to my late father, Glenn K. Gunderson Sr.,
who heard "Well done, good and faithful servant!"
on July 5, 1999.
Outside of God's Word, these two people have been
my most wonderful antidotes to life's toxins.*

CONTENTS

Preface   ix

Acknowledgments   xi

Chapter 1:   THE GREAT PHYSICIAN   1

Chapter 2:   TOXIC STRESS   9

Chapter 3:   TOXIC INFERIORITY   23

Chapter 4:   TOXIC LONELINESS   39

Chapter 5:   TOXIC ANGER   53

Chapter 6:   TOXIC DISCOURAGEMENT   69

Chapter 7:   TOXIC JEALOUSY   83

Chapter 8:   TOXIC WORRY   95

Chapter 9:   TOXIC RESENTMENT   109

Chapter 10:   TOXIC TEMPTATION   123

Chapter 11:   TOXIC DEPRESSION   137

Chapter 12:   TOXIC FEAR   149

Chapter 13:   TOXIC EXPECTATIONS   163

Chapter 14:   THE ULTIMATE ANTIDOTE   175

Notes   177

Preface

My wife, Kimberly, and I had just finished speaking at a marriage conference in upstate New York. Our topic was "Biblical Antidotes to Marriage Toxins." Once again, we realized the relevance of God's Word to people struggling with stress, discouragement, and fear. Normally, we would have flown from New York back to Los Angeles on that Tuesday morning, but I was officiating at my nephew's wedding in Washington, D.C., later that week.

The date was September 11, 2001.

As the tragic events of that day unfolded, people throughout the United States called out to God for strength, help, and comfort. How do you handle the stress of events outside of your control? How do you deal with the anger caused by injustice, the worries about your future? What about resentment, fear, discouragement, and loneliness in the face of life's harshness? God says through the prophet Jeremiah, "Call to me, and I will answer you . . ." (Jer 33:3).

On Saturday, September 15, I sat alone on a bench on the Washington, D.C., mall and called out to God for our country. It was eerie to see the city's downtown practically deserted. But already one could see signs that life would go on. My nephew was married the night before. The bride's father walked his daughter down the aisle, even though he worked in the Pentagon, near to where the hijacked airliner had struck. He had taken the week off for the wedding preparations and was not at his desk that tragic Tuesday morning.

It turned out that Kimberly and I were stranded for several days in D.C. until we could find a flight back to Los Angeles. Eventually we returned home, and here, too, life continued.

A few months later, I spoke at a Bible conference in New Jersey and visited the site of the attack in New York City. The cleanup and recovery was almost complete, the internal hurts were beginning to heal, and Manhattan was again a bustling city.

It is possible to recover from life's hurts and toxins. It takes time and the touch of the Great Physician, but it can happen. Sometimes it takes a health crisis to get us to the doctor. Sometimes it takes a spiritual crisis to get us to the Great Physician. My prayer for you, as you read this book, is that you will once again find hope: Hope that you can recover. Hope that you can heal. Hope that you can continue. Hope that you can find antidotes to life's toxins in the pages of the Great Physician's medical manual—the Bible.

Acknowledgments

THIS BOOK TRULY represents the cooperative efforts of many people working together. Many thanks to Kathy Gisi Wimbish for offering her time and writing skills to make this book a reality. She has taken my ideas and crafted them into a readable form with great expertise and diligence. Without her, this project would not have happened. I can't thank her enough. A special word of appreciation goes to Beverly Moudy and Florence Mellard, my extremely competent, ever-faithful executive assistants for their research and behind-the-scenes service. I also wish to thank David Wimbish for his editorial guidance and advice, and Christopher Dacus for his diligent help in transcribing tapes. I also thank David Hazard of Hazard Communications, Inc., for his help and guidance in the production of an earlier, privately distributed version of this book.

The church family of First Baptist Church of Pomona, California, also deserves my applause. As I teach, week by week, their thirst for God's Word and desire to apply it in practical ways inspires and encourages me. I am so blessed to be their pastor.

My most special thanks, as always, goes to my family. My wife, Kimberly, is such a wonderful source of emotional strength and support for me personally. My children—John, Andrew, Abby, Leah, Rebekah, and Noah—are the joy of my life and are such good sports about being the subject of many of my illustrations. (It helps that I pay them a dollar for each time I mention them in a sermon. Maybe for this book I'd better up the rate to ten dollars per reference.)

And finally, my hope and prayer is that this book will honor my dear Lord and Savior, Jesus Christ, and also help people to experience fully the abundant "toxin-free" life He came to give.

Chapter 1

The Great Physician

ॐ

*Call to Me, and
I will answer you . . .*

—JER 33:3 (NKJV)

ॐ

RUN, RUN, RUN. Some days it seems to Mary that she's living on a treadmill and she can't reach the off switch.

There was a time when she worked hard at filling up her schedule. Now she'd die for half an hour with nothing to do. Mary can't let up on herself. Run to work. Run to Little League practice. Run to the PTA meeting. She can't cut back.

After all, what kind of mom would she be if she didn't do her part? Never mind that she's always tired and that almost every word she speaks to her kids is laced with irritation. Never mind that her quiet time with God is on hold. The joy and peace she used to feel is gone and she doesn't know why.

Recognize the symptoms? Mary is stressed out.

ॐ   ॐ   ॐ

It's only 5 A.M. on a Saturday morning, but John has been awake for hours, trying to escape the relentless fear that fragments every night into a series of bad dreams and panic attacks. About a year ago he hurt his back at work. Physical therapy helped but the pain keeps coming back. John is afraid to tell his boss. What would happen to his wife and sons if he couldn't work any more? Already collection agents are calling because he has fallen behind on his bill payments. What if the bank forecloses? What if . . . what if . . . what if? Recognize worry? John has a classic case.

᪥ ᪥ ᪥

Traci is a senior in high school. She remembers when her sister, Jen, was a senior. She was the prettiest girl at the prom, and colleges were fighting over her. Mom and Dad were so proud. Traci was determined to be like Jen.

But Traci wasn't invited to the prom, and when she took her SATs, her mind kept going blank. Her scores were only average. She'll never get into any of the colleges on her list. If only she were prettier and smarter, like Jen. Maybe then her parents would be proud of her.

What's the use? She hasn't told anybody, but Traci often thinks about dying. It would be easier than trying to live up to everyone's expectations—especially her own.

What's wrong with Traci? Her low self-esteem and high expectations are to her as deadly as poison.

᪥ ᪥ ᪥

Mary, John, and Traci are examples of people who are suffering from the effects of what I call "spiritual toxins." I'll explain what I mean by that shortly, but first, consider this question: *What would you do if you accidentally ingested a dangerous amount of a poisonous substance?*

Seems like a simple question, doesn't it? Of course, you'd rush to the phone and call 911. In fact, you may have even anticipated just such an emergency by placing a sticker on your phone that is printed with an emergency hot-line number. By dialing into the number, you'd immediately access a trained poison-control expert who would advise you to take the proper antidote to halt the toxin's imminent threat to your life and health. The counselor would urge you to visit a hospital emergency room or to contact your personal physician for further medical advice and any required treatment.

You may be thinking, "That was a no-brainer." The answer to the question is simple common sense, isn't it?

But let me ask you another question. If you knew your spirit was fading within you from the effects of a crippling spiritual poison, what would you do then? The answer is not quite as obvious, is it?

Spiritual growth and change is not as tangible. Yet, there are "spiritual toxins" that are equally as deadly to your well-being as any poisonous substance you might breathe or ingest into your body.

In fact, these spiritual toxins are even *more* lethal because they attack your soul. They undermine your relationship with God and with the people you love. And they are far more insidious, seeping into your mind and heart and stealing away the powerful, productive life that Jesus came to give you.

You're probably wondering what I mean by "spiritual toxins." They are not the things that seem obvious to you—such as cults, hardships, addictions, or religious persecution. Certainly these are very real and ominous threats. As Christians, we expect Satan to attack us through these avenues, and because they are obvious, we are more likely to stay on guard, ready to combat these enemies.

When I speak of spiritual toxins, I'm talking about emotions and experiences such as stress, loneliness, jealousy, depression, and many others. These experiences are so much a part of daily life that we accept them and take them for granted. Left unchecked, however, these feelings can spiral out of control and become abnormal and unhealthy. They can grow in intensity until they stifle our soul and rob us of inner peace and joy. They can render us ineffective as Christians, and that's when they become "toxic."

As we hurt and grieve and limp through life, we may try to ignore what's happening—just as we sometimes ignore annoying, chronic physical symptoms. By pushing them aside, perhaps we think they'll simply go away. But to take this approach is almost like tolling our own death bell. These emotional and spiritual poisons, if denied, will eventually quench the Holy Spirit and render us lifeless and useless to God, to others, and to ourselves.

King David was a man who struggled throughout his life with spiritual toxins. Anxiety, depression, loneliness, temptation—the pages of David's story are filled with mention of the issues he wrestled with. But he apparently understood the importance of dealing with them by bringing them out into the open before God. "Cleanse me from secret faults," he cried to his Maker. "Keep back Your servant also from presumptuous sins; let them not have dominion over me" (Ps 19:13, NKJV).

I admire the way David opened himself to God. Sometimes we have a tendency to do just the opposite. We suppress our problems and put on a happy face to hide our negative emotions. Of course, they are not hidden from God. And if we continue to deny them to ourselves, they erode our faith and spiritual strength.

As we try to hide from God, we also attempt to take life into our own hands. Eventually, we become so like the world around us that we cease to stand out. At this point, if we aren't careful, we can become pawns of Satan, who is delighted to find us in a depleted spiritual state. Because Christ owns us, Satan can't have our soul. But he will surely jump in and use our resentment, anger, worry, or any other "poison" he can find to make us look sick and unattractive to others he is trying so desperately to claim.

Let me stress that it is inevitable that we will experience fatigue. Stress will get hold of us. Anxiety and worry will plague us. As we go through life, emotions and experiences such as these are to be expected. They can even make us stronger as we rely on God to help us deal with them.

But heed this word of caution. Spiritual struggles can turn into toxic poisons when they become habitual. It's not the occasional drink that makes a person an alcoholic. Neither is it the normal, everyday worries, stress, or fear that rob us of our spiritual health. That's why we must be on guard, because the normal can grow to be abnormal if we are not careful.

If this is happening in your life, I have good news for you. You have a Great Physician who is ready and waiting to prescribe powerful antidotes that will renew and restore you. Immediate, direct access is available through prayer—wherever you are, whenever you need to "dial in." The Lord is always there, standing by, ready and anxious to answer.

God's reply to our prayers often comes through healing words that are readily available to us in the Bible. But I don't want to mislead you. *The Bible is not a quick fix for our problems.*

I have a friend who was diagnosed several years ago with high blood pressure. Her doctor prescribed medication, which she took for a while. Then she began to feel better. She wasn't very old, after all. Maybe it was a fluke. So she stopped taking the blood pressure medication. For a while, she was fine. Then some strange symptoms surfaced that drove her back to the doctor. Her blood pressure was dangerously high, and he ordered tests to see if her vital organs had been damaged.

I'm glad to report that my friend responded to her symptoms in time, and that she learned a valuable lesson. In order to safeguard her health, she had to adhere to the treatment plan her doctor prescribed. She had to accept it, embrace it, and be committed to it—for the rest of her life.

The remainder of this book will offer you a preventative treatment plan to help you safeguard your spiritual health. It's a tried and true plan—but it's not a quick fix. You must be committed to the plan for the rest of your life in order for it to have the spiritual impact God intends.

As you read the chapters that follow, you'll learn about twelve common spiritual toxins that jeopardize Christian vitality. Together, we'll look at what they are and examine the debilitating effects they have on our relationships with God and with other people. We'll also identify the scriptural remedies available to stop these toxins from draining the spiritual life out of us.

Some preventative measures are suggested in each chapter to help you incorporate what you've learned into your own daily spiritual health regimen. If you follow the measures, you will begin to experience the benefits of spiritual health that God wants you to enjoy. His peace, joy, and serenity will renew and refresh you. You will experience the abundant life He promised you. And you will also become an increasingly more effective witness for Christ.

Now let me help you begin by encouraging you to take the following simple steps now:

Get alone with God and with yourself. In the quiet intimacy of your prayers, open your heart honestly and expectantly. Ask God to help you name the toxins that are jeopardizing your spiritual health. Write them in the space provided at the end of this chapter.

Admit that you need a treatment plan. Ask God to use this book (and other resources He will reveal) to help you develop one. Begin by setting aside a prescribed time every day to meet with Him for your personal treatment.

Put aside your inhibitions. If you feel guilty or ashamed, ask God to help you reject these barriers. Remember that there is "no condemnation to those who are in Christ Jesus . . . who do not walk according to the flesh, but according to the Spirit" (Rom 8:1, 4, NKJV).

The first step is always the hardest. I urge you to take that step today by asking the Great Physician for His help and guidance. There's no better time than now.

Applying the Antidote

Take a moment now to "diagnose" your spiritual condition. Fill in the blanks below and ask God to use this book to help you find the best biblical antidote for the "poisoned" places in your life.

Diagnosis:

The dangerous spiritual toxins in my life are:

1. _____

2. _____

3. _____

For: Life's Toxins

"O Lord, your discipline is good and leads to life and health. Oh, heal me and make me live!"

—Isa 38:16 (TLB)

Toxic
Stress

RUSH HOUR. Jerry inches down the freeway toward home. What a day. The client presentation he's been preparing for weeks didn't go so well. He has a splitting headache and a knot in his stomach. As traffic grinds to a halt, Jerry pops antacids like peanuts. Suddenly he hears an alarming noise and the car begins to jerk. Blowout! With a sinking heart, Jerry pulls over to change the tire. Looks like he'll have to bypass home altogether and head straight for that committee meeting at church.

Meanwhile, at home, Jerry's wife, Claire, pulls into the carport at home. Her day has been much like Jerry's, except she lucked out in traffic. She's already been by the day-care center, stopped at the dry cleaners, and driven through McDonalds to purchase two Happy Meals, three Big Macs, and four large fries, which have been nearly devoured by Danny and Melissa. Claire tries to be cheerful as she directs the kids to change clothes and to grab their backpacks so they can start their homework on the way to soccer practice. She feeds the dog, flips through the mail and herds everyone back into the car. Then off they go—again. Two hours later Jerry, Claire, and the kids all drag into the house tired, frazzled, and more than a little bit on edge. Three nights in a row of cold burgers and fries aren't Jerry's idea of home cooking. Danny and Melissa bicker, as usual, over who gets to use the phone first. And Claire's impersonation of a martyr could win her an Oscar.

Got stress? I bet you have. The scene I've just described is as American as baseball, apple pie, and the Green Bay Packers. Most of us recognize the above as an example of simple, ordinary, everyday stress. As a parent of six busy kids and pastor of a growing church, I can relate to Jerry and Claire's hectic lifestyle. I think if someone were to ask me to describe life in suburban America, the first word that would come to my mind is *stress*.

Psychologists tell us that stress does not always have a negative impact. In fact, there is good stress and bad, and we actually need a little of the good kind to keep us motivated and to add excitement to life. The good kind of stress even has a name. It's called "eustress."

Sometimes stress is a necessary by-product of activities and commitments that we take on to enrich and broaden our lives. I remember a Gunderson family vacation my wife, Kimberly, and I planned in an attempt to escape from our daily stress—a vacation that turned out to be anything but stress-free. However, it did leave us with a very interesting memory.

This particular vacation was a winter getaway. We were living in New York at the time and the temperature outside was hanging right around ten degrees. I thought it would be easier (and much warmer) to drive the car into the garage and pack it there. Sounds logical, wouldn't you say? It made complete sense to me.

We were leaving right after church on a Sunday morning, so I loaded the carrier the night before. I climbed in bed that night feeling pretty proud of myself for my efficiency and advance planning.

Morning found me tearing around in a frenzy. Late for church, I threw on some clothes, grabbed an apple as I flew through the kitchen, jumped in my car, and started the ignition. As I backed out of the garage I heard a terrible screeching noise—much to my dismay—the kind that causes your heart to skip a few beats. What could be happening?

The answer came to me in a rush—the proverbial "light bulb" went on in my head. Suddenly I realized there was enough clearance in our garage to pack the carrier inside, but not to get the car and carrier *out* of the garage.

I jumped out of the car and started tossing things out of the carrier left and right. In a matter of seconds, the garage looked like an airport baggage terminal on the Sunday after Thanksgiving. Finally, I ripped the carrier itself off and proceeded on to church. Even though I was long gone, I could clearly picture the look on Kimberly's face when she stepped into the garage a short while later. It's a look I've seen more than a few times.

But that's not the end of my story.

Now I know that an experience like this would have been enough to teach most people a lesson. But it wasn't enough for me. On our next vacation, we made it safely out of the garage and were already cruising toward a good time. If only we hadn't stopped to get gas at a place that offered a free car wash (the kind where you drive through a giant contraption that bombards your vehicle with soap, water, and giant brushes) with every fill-up.

Perhaps a thought is occurring to you at this very moment, a thought that *should* have occurred to me. But it didn't, and so we proceeded with what turned out to be the nightmare of all car washes. Yes, it was that clearance thing again. We were able to drive into the car wash fine, but once inside, we got stuck.

At first we couldn't figure out what was wrong. We hung there with brushes thumping and crashing all around us, feeling embarrassed and fearing that a crowd was gathering to point and stare. Suddenly the light bulb went on again: Kimberly and I turned to each other and said, "The car-top carrier!"

With our carrier crushed and battered, we finally maneuvered our way out of the foaming mass of brushes. Mortified and frustrated, all I could think to do was to floor the accelerator and flee the scene.

Needless to say, I'm not even going to tell you about our *next* vacation.

I've shared my car-carrier stories with you, at great expense to my male ego, to emphasize the point that even things we do to relax can be stressful. Stress is simply unavoidable, and it's not realistic—or even desirable—to think we can totally eliminate it from our lives. But when stress gets out of control and becomes unmanageable, it ceases to be "eustress" (good stress) and becomes "distress" (bad stress.)

Thousands of Americans suffer from some kind of stress-related illness during the course of a year. To determine how stress is affecting a person, psychologists often use a questionnaire called the Holmes-Rahe Stress Test. In scoring this test, a numeric value is assessed for a variety of events or experiences a person is undergoing, or has undergone in recent weeks. The test is used to indicate how "at-risk" a person is to develop physical illness, depression, or to have difficulties in interpersonal relationships.

According to experts, stressful situations are not all bad. However, they all involve change, and too much change, too close in time, causes stress to go out of control. Stress can cause us to lose our temper. It can make us forgetful and disorganized. How many times have you done something crazy because you were "on-the-fly," and then felt foolish?

Because stress is so common in our lives, the threat it can pose to our well-being is camouflaged by its normalcy. And if we are not careful, stress can gradually and insidiously intensify until it is out of control. At this point, it can harm us psychologically, physically, and spiritually.

Alex was a successful top-level executive in the automobile industry. From the first day he started as a young clerk in the mailroom, he had worked with energy, zeal, and ambition to climb the corporate ladder. With each promotion, he was proud and pleased.

His job became the measuring rod for his self-worth as he devoted himself to providing a secure, rich life for his growing family.

Year by year, life became increasingly fast-paced and hectic. Time was slipping away, and while Alex was out on the road handling business, he sometimes felt as if he were watching his children through a telescope. Although his children were of utmost importance to him, his job didn't allow him to be there to share many of their experiences first-hand. There were months when he was home only two short weekends, barely long enough to read through the mail. He was tired and downhearted, and even though he had been a Christian since childhood, Alex felt just as distant from God as he did from his wife and children.

He became increasingly restless and prone to bouts of depression. One day, while sitting on his bed pulling on his socks, a flood of tears streamed down his face. Stress was eating away at him, body and soul. His work, once such a joy, was now a dark, heavy burden. Every day, getting out of bed was harder and harder. Still, he pushed himself to keep going.

Then late one night, driving home on the freeway after a big company event, Alex blacked out at the wheel of his car. Just before he lost consciousness, he sensed something was happening and drove to the shoulder and stopped. When he awoke, he was in a hospital bed. All he could do was lie there and think while the doctors ran tests. He took that time to pray, sincerely and openly, that God would take control and show him what to do. That's when he realized that toxic stress had him by the throat, and that it might literally take his life unless he made some changes.

Not long after this incident, Alex turned in his letter of resignation. He had no idea what he would do for the rest of his life, or how he would support his family. But he renewed his practice of daily Bible study and prayer, and God soon began to show him what to do.

The blackout on the freeway became a catalyst to a new life in a new place where God used Alex in fruitful ways for the rest of his life. When he died, just a few months shy of his eightieth birthday, the church overflowed with people of all ages who came to express their gratitude for Alex's zeal in sharing God's Word and for his exemplary Christian life.

Life's stress points can be turning points. If we respond as Alex did to God's warnings, stress can steer us into His will and open doors to fruitful ministry.

Is stress spinning out of control in your life? Be comforted. As He did for Alex, God may be directing you toward the most productive, meaningful time of your life. So don't be afraid. His Word offers practical guidelines to help you control toxic stress.

Before we examine those guidelines, let's identify some of the major causes of stress, since the first step to addressing a problem is to understand where it's coming from.

The Ultimate Setup: Unrealistic Expectations

Many of us are under pressure from a lot of different sources. At home, at work, even in the discretionary activities and friendships in our lives, we're expected to be on top of a complex jumble of things at all times. We are seduced by the media, buying into messages such as the one conveyed by a famous beer commercial that tells us, "You can have it all."

But we *can't* have it all. We *can't* do it all. We *can't* be it all.

To expect that we can have it, do it, and be it all is totally unrealistic. As life unfolds, you learn you can successfully invest yourself in certain areas and not others. You realize you can do a number of things with excellence, but you can't do *everything* and expect the same quality of performance from yourself. Those who do expect to do it all are headed for trouble in the form of nervous breakdown, stress-related illness, depression, and more. You don't have to be a spiritual old-timer to know that these are not conditions God approves of or desires for His children.

Superman—or Super-Ego?

Another source of unhealthy stress lies in the quest to satisfy deep-seated yearnings to be important. The society we live in, the way we are raised, and our emotional needs predispose us to the mistaken belief that our worth as individuals is somehow directly proportional to our accomplishments. We try to pile up accomplishments that can validate our importance. We volunteer for chairman of every committee at church. We're coaches of Little League and soccer teams, room mothers, Girl Scout leaders—we work into the night and on weekends trying to climb the corporate ladder. You name it, we do it.

You may be saying, "Those things you just listed are good things, aren't they? Doesn't God want us to direct our personal gifts, talents, and energy into activities and accomplishments that fill our lives with meaning? Aren't we supposed to be blessing others through our activities?"

Of course God wants you to grow and develop and be busy. As long as He is at the center of your life, directing you and using you, your achievements will be fulfilling and rewarding—a blessing to you and to others. However, from time to time it's essential to look deep within yourself to analyze priorities and activities. And when you do, you may have to admit that many of your involvements have been assumed not because they are God's desire, but because the needs of your ego drives you to find tangible proofs of your importance.

Hard Times: That's Life

Someone once said, "If we didn't expect life to be so easy, it wouldn't be so hard."

Hard times are as much a part of life as good times. Part of the problem is that we tell ourselves, "Life is not supposed to be hard." So when difficulties and stress arise, they catch us off-guard. Hard times would be easier to cope with if we would expect them to happen from time to time and prepare ourselves mentally and emotionally to roll with the punches. When we accept and acknowledge that life is a series of ups and downs and ask God to help us manage the burdens that fall on us, they are amazingly less stressful.

You see, God allows hard times to happen because He wants to build us into strong, victorious people with a faith that is equally muscular. Even though we do not look forward to our seasons of suffering, in retrospect we often see how God used them as conduits for His power and glory. Often we shine brightest for Him when darkness engulfs us. If we embrace this spiritual principle ahead of time, it's easier to swallow life's most bitter pill.

Jesus Never Promised a Rose Garden

Have you ever known someone who seemed to have it all: good health, financial security, a great family, material possessions, the whole package? And then he came face-to-face with Jesus, accepted Him as his Savior, and problems started falling on him left and right?

Jesus never said it would be easy to be a Christian. In fact, a decision to follow Jesus starts an unseen war between God and His enemy, Satan, because Satan has lost another soul, and he's not a good loser. Once a person joins God's army, Satan will do everything he possibly can to distract, disarm, and discolor that person's witness and to discredit Jesus Christ. It's called "spiritual warfare," and it can be very stressful.

Once again, we shouldn't be surprised. The apostle Peter says, "Dear friends, do not be surprised at the painful trial you are suffering as though something strange were happening to you" (2 Pet 4:12). As believers in Jesus, taking a stand for righteousness—a stand for Christ in this day and age—we can expect stress and pressure due to spiritual warfare.

The good news is that God sent Jesus to show us how to conduct our lives, and He has provided everything we need for victorious living. It's all right there in His Word, the Bible. So now let's take a look at four practical biblical principles—or treatment plans, if you will—that can help us to effectively manage and direct the stress in our lives.

Prescription #1: Preventive Prayer

A couple of thousand years ago on an ordinary day, a crowd of people with all kinds of problems came searching for Jesus. These men, women, and children were sick in body and soul. Some were even possessed by demons. They were stressed. They had heard about this man, Jesus, who could perform miracles. As they flocked to Him, He went up onto a mountainside and gave them a crash course in Christian living. He hit on just about every topic you could think of for life's textbook, including anxiety over "things."

"But seek first His kingdom and His righteousness," He said, "and all these things will given to you as well" (Matt 6:33). Sounds so simple, doesn't it? And it is, if we really trust God. When we come before Him and sincerely ask for His assistance in aligning our priorities with His, He promises that other things will fall into place and our life will become more manageable.

I love 1 Tim 6:19, which says in part, "take hold of the life that is truly life." Let's invest ourselves in the real thing. Imagine if you had a gift certificate to spend $1 million at a local department store. You wouldn't have to think much about what to buy. One million dollars would go far enough to buy everything you could ever need or want.

But life is not like having $1 million to spend at a department store. It's more like having $100 to spend. And that's an entirely different story. With only $100, you would have to think much more carefully and critically before making each and every purchase. Even though $100 can purchase something nice, it can't buy everything you'd ever need or want. You would have to make choices.

That's the way life is, too. You can't have it all, do it all, possess it all. You have to make hard decisions and say, "I choose to invest myself in this, and not that." A friend of mine once said, "Nothing lasts for eternity except two things—people and the Word of God." I've thought a great deal about that statement, and I believe there is a lot of truth to it. If we invest time in reading and applying God's Word to our lives and in cultivating solid, godly relationships, those investments will pay eternal rewards. We will be able to look back and be pleased that we embraced things that will last for eternity, rather than embracing fleeting pleasures and possessions.

As you pray about your priorities, ask God to impart to you His wisdom. In a graduation speech, former first lady Barbara Bush challenged students with the following words:

> *At the end of your life, you will never regret not having passed one more test, winning one more verdict, or not closing one more deal. You will regret time not spent with a husband, a child, a friend, or a parent.*[1]

How true. Work-related activities are important and they may put bread on the table, but we have to be careful not to become so consumed by them that we miss out on building relationships with God and with one another.

Prescription #2: Get Plenty of Rest

Early in His relationship with mankind, God made it clear that we should take time to rest. "Six days you shall labor, but on the seventh day you shall rest," He commands. And then He adds, "Even during the plowing season and harvest, you must rest" (Exod 34:21).

Isn't that good news? Rest isn't a luxury. It's not a self-centered indulgence. It's not even an option. God commands us to rest, even during the busiest times. This is the "sabbath principle," and we need to heed it as carefully as we would take the advice of a doctor if we were being treated for a serious illness. In the long run, we work and perform best when we obey this principle, even when special needs require hours of overtime—even when there's a special project at home, and especially when we are tempted to think we can't take time to rest.

I can't overemphasize the importance of applying the discipline of biblical rest. Our "go-go-go" society constantly tempts you to pare down the amount of time you spend sleeping and renewing your body, mind, and soul. Yet rest is the very tool you need to perform optimally. And lack of it on a regular basis will surely cause burnout, or worse.

Prescription #3: Know Thyself

A third principle for managing stress is to cultivate the practice of "critical thinking." This has nothing to do with criticizing other people. It means that in all we do we need to ask ourselves, "Why am I doing what I am doing? Why am I taking this on?" The apostle Paul warned, "Be very careful, then, how you live—not as unwise but as wise, making the most of every opportunity, because the days are evil. Therefore do not be foolish, but understand what the Lord's will is" (Eph 5:15–17). If we pray about our priorities and take good care of ourselves by getting adequate rest, we'll be able to focus on God's guidance as He offers it to us. We'll be able to apply critical thinking to the choices we make.

I find that January is not the starting point of the year for the Gundersons. For us, it's the Tuesday after Labor Day. This is when we begin to think about what we're going to be involved in as we launch into a whole new year of school and extracurricular activities. This is when we need to stop and say, "Lord, why are we doing this? Is this something that meets your long-range goals for us, or are we just yielding to short-term pressure?"

In order to talk to God like this, you have to set aside time to be alone with Him. A regular, daily "quiet time" is something we ought never to neglect, no matter how busy each day is. There are two things that I like to take into my daily appointment with the Lord. One is my Bible, to help me get my mind thinking His thoughts. The other is my planner. After I've spent some time in the Word, I open it and ask, "Lord, show me now where You'd have me invest my time. What would You have me plan for today, and the rest of this week and beyond?" This helps me to analyze my priorities and activities, to make sure I know why I'm doing what I'm doing.

Prescription #4: You Can't Overdose on Prayer

You know that expression, "Too much of a good thing can be a bad thing"? Not with prayer. And where stress is concerned, prayer needs to be taken in large doses at frequent intervals. In 1 Thes 5:17, we are told to "pray without ceasing." This doesn't mean we should hide in a closet, on our knees, twenty-four hours a day. It means that prayer should be as natural as breathing to us.

Ponder these practical words from God:

> Do not be anxious about anything, but in everything, by prayer and petition, with thanksgiving, present your requests to God. And the peace of God, which transcends all understanding, will guard your hearts and your minds in Christ Jesus. (Phil 4:6–7, NIV)

By keeping this scripture in mind, we can build a powerful, practical reaction that can be applied over and over again in times of anxiety and stress. Instantly, we can take this before the Lord in an attitude of prayer. "Lord, this thing that is stressing me out I want to submit to you immediately. I place it in Your care and ask that You help me to manage it effectively, so it can work *for* me, rather than tear my emotions and spirit down." This is a constructive response to stress. Most of us adopt a more destructive approach, letting anxiety simmer within us until it boils over and our lives are out of control.

The Bottom Line

Are you tired? Worn out? Is stress out of control in your life? Jesus extends a compelling invitation to you today: "Come to me, all you who are weary and burdened, and I will give you rest" (Matt 11:28).

Jesus is more than able to help cure what ails you. And, you don't have to wait three weeks for an appointment. Any time, day or night, right this very minute, you can go to His Word for help.

But just as antibiotics won't do you any good if you fail to take them as prescribed, neither will God's biblical principles help you unless you apply them on a regular basis to your life.

Why not start right now? On the next page, you'll find an "offloading" stress prayer written by David Mains. I challenge you to pray it often, identifying the particular stressors that are most burdensome to you. As you do, expect God to help you. I think the results will surprise you.

Applying the Antidote

Off-Loading Stress Prayer
by David Mains

"Father, You are God, even in stress-filled time. On my own I could feel overwhelmed, but scripture tells me You care about every detail of my life. Right now, the stress I feel most intensely is (insert your personal stressors):

_____

_____

"Show me the steps I can take, and give me the courage to take them. Calm my spirit, Lord, as I trust You to bring good in this situation. Amen."[2]

For: Stress

"Give your burdens to the Lord. He will carry them. He will not permit the godly to slip or fall."

—Ps 55:22 (TLB)

Chapter 3

Toxic Inferiority

ॐ

Just as I am,
without one plea,
But that Thy blood
was shed for me.

—CHARLOTTE ELLIOTT

ॐ

IT WAS HER TIME to shine. Graceful, elegant, controlled—American figure skater Michelle Kwan, seemed to draw warmth and life out of the cold, hard ice as she skated her final program at the 1998 Winter Olympic Games. For years she had been training and competing, sacrificing the carefree freedom of childhood to pursue her goal. Her mind and heart were focused on one purpose—to win the gold medal in the women's figure skating Olympic competition.

As she glided over the ice, her face was radiant. Each time she landed a difficult jump, her soul seemed to soar. At the end of her program, in perfect precision with the dwindling musical notes, Michelle skated to a stop—and the crowd went wild. Reporters and judges alike affirmed her with glowing words and near perfect scores. It certainly appeared at that moment that Michelle would go home with the coveted gold medal. How could anyone beat her performance?

And yet, just a few hours later when photographers cornered Michelle backstage, her face was no longer radiant. She fought back tears and struggled for the gracious poise that was her signature.

Though she tried hard to hide it, her disappointment was unmistakable. According to the judges, her American teammate, Tara Lipinski, had skated just a little bit better. Michelle would not be the gold medalist after all.

Here's what's amazing. As reporters talked with Michelle, the same elegance and grace that had defined her program also defined her responses. She deliberately projected a positive attitude, even though her feelings of regret came through as she talked about the silver medal almost as if it were tarnished. She stood before the camera as one of the world's top-three women's figure skaters, but she was apologetic for not being number one.

In figure skating—and in life—nobody's perfect. We all know that. If our value was contingent upon being number one, 99 percent of us would fall short.

Yet perfection is something we seem to expect from ourselves and from others. And when we fail to meet the high standard we have set, rather than applauding ourselves for coming so close and acknowledging what a victory it was just to try, we sink into feelings of failure and low self-esteem.

Olympic medallists, the president of the United States, doctors, lawyers, teachers, adults, and children alike—no one is immune to feelings of inferiority. In fact, it is surprisingly true that people with the least reason to feel inferior are often the ones most prone toward feelings of inadequacy.

Psychologists have discovered a correlation between IQ and vulnerability to low self-esteem. Ironically, it seems people of high intelligence are the ones most likely to struggle with this issue. Sometimes people like this put on a psychological mask and project a superior attitude. They package what they say in cynicism and sarcasm. From all outward appearances, we'd never suspect that they have feelings of self-doubt. But in truth, they do. And their words are used to hide insecurity and a lack of self-confidence.

Pride Goes before a Fall

Not long ago, a "self-esteem movement" took hold in our society. Many people in the Christian community were offended by its philosophy, which stated that the solution to low self-esteem could be found in self-sufficiency. However, God warns us that this attribute does *not* earn His approval or blessing, even though society tries to convince us that feelings of inferiority can be overcome through independence, self-confidence, and self-reliance.

It's easy to be taken in by this way of thinking, since advertising and the media feed it to us over the airwaves and even on billboards we pass while driving to work each day. The message is loud and clear: Be an island unto yourself. Master your own universe. Look out for number one. As we try to conform to the message, we might find it actually works for a while. But eventually the mask starts to slip and the truth becomes unavoidable. If we are honest and realistic, we must acknowledge that we are not independent, nor are we totally self-sufficient.

The New Age movement would have us believe that we are all "little gods"—individual "suns" at the center of our own private solar systems, with everything and everybody revolving around us. What a burden it would be to always have to have everything under control. Scripture teaches that we were not created to spin in our own orbits. God designed us to be more like the planets, rightly aligned with Him—the one, true, Living God.

Centuries ago, Augustine wrote: "Our hearts are restless, O God, until they find their rest in Thee." Many of us can add our personal "amen" to this testimony. We have struggled and wrestled and burned ourselves out trying to find happiness within ourselves, only to discover instead that fulfillment resides in surrender and submission. As the saying goes, "Let go and let God." That's the only effective antidote for toxic feelings of inferiority, and it is only when we apply it that we fully realize how much God values and cherishes us.

The Problem with Inferiority

We face and interesting problem when we struggle to overcome feelings of inferiority. Though it sounds like a contradiction, feelings of inferiority are rooted in self-centeredness. As we focus on comparing ourselves to others, we also give into another dangerous tendency. We wallow in self-pity; the more we wallow, the more focused we become on "self."

I'm going to tell you a principle that may seem to be a little off-target: To develop healthy self-esteem, you must forget yourself. You see, low self-esteem is an outgrowth of focusing too much on self and too little on Christ. As we change this habit and focus increasingly on Him, He imparts to us the attributes that drew us to Him. And the more we are like Him, the better we feel about ourselves.

We can liken this to taking off soiled clothes and putting on new, spotless garments. This is what Paul meant when he said, "Set your minds on things above, not on earthly things. For you died, and your life is now hidden with Christ in God" (Col 3:2–3). As we become increasingly practiced at this, we reflect the character of Christ. That's when we will have healthy self-esteem, because we will feel good about who we are.

A Dose of Humility Can Have Dramatic Results

To reflect Christ's character, we must first come to the end of ourselves. We must, in effect, become humble.

Many people confuse the positive attribute of *humility* with the negative condition of *humiliation*. Close your eyes and think of a time when you felt humiliated. Maybe you're thinking about that day when you worked hard to prepare a presentation, and your boss criticized your strategy in front of your fellow employees and an important client.

Or maybe you are going way back to that day in third grade when you were the very last kid to be chosen as the baseball captains selected their teams. Remember feeling stupid, inadequate, bad, rejected, humiliated? You felt like you were under a spotlight, didn't you? When you think about it, feelings of humiliation are very self-focused.

Humility, on the other hand, is God-focused. It comes when we assume our proper place in God's universal order. We are no longer *performing* under a spotlight that places us at the center of attention. We are simply doing what He created us to do.

The humility that God describes in His Word is a mark of His glory at work through us. In Rom 12:3 we are admonished not to think of ourselves more highly than we ought. We are not self-made people. Each of us is God's creation, fashioned and designed through His creative genius. Any achievements or successes we enjoy in our life should put Him in the spotlight. Paul reminds us that we are "the body of Christ" (1 Cor 12:27). As we reflect His glory, we also *share* it because we are in Him. Do you see the difference between being humiliated by our own self-directed works and being humbled by His glorious acts through us?

Spoiled by Sin

When Adam and Eve made a choice to sin, God's creative masterpiece—mankind—became inherently flawed. And ever since, each human being has been born into the world as a complex mass of strengths and weaknesses. When we recognize this, it's the first step toward balanced self-esteem.

Gary Collins has said that "humility involves a grateful dependence on God and a realistic appraisal of both our strengths and weaknesses." Aren't you glad you can depend on God? I know I would be scared stiff if I had to face each day in my own strength.

Thankfully, I have a loving, powerful, heavenly Father to depend on for strength, competence, and insight. And so do you!

As a Christian, I'm also grateful that weaknesses are not something we have to hide or suppress. We can actually affirm those weaknesses, knowing that God created us to be just the way we are, with a unique set of personality traits. In Rom 8:28 He promises to bring good to His children through all things. *All* things—even our weaknesses. There's no disclaimer at the end of Romans 8 that says "excluded from this promise is Glenn Gunderson." His promise is for each and every one of His saved children—and that includes you and me. When we realize that almighty God assures us that *everything* concerning us will be used by Him for some good purpose and for His glory, it opens the door to the kind of serene happiness that Jesus wants us to have.

Three Biblical Case Histories

Low self-esteem that leads to self-centeredness is not a modern condition. Scripture includes many case histories of real people who were crippled by feelings of inadequacy, until they came to God for the antidote. Let's look at three of these people.

Moses

Remember Moses? His case history can be found in chapters 3 and 4 of the book of Exodus. Here's a brief recap of those chapters:

One day while tending his father-in-law's sheep, Moses comes across a bush that is aflame, but not being consumed. God's voice calls out to Moses from the burning bush, telling him that His heart is stirred by the plight of the Israelites who are cruelly enslaved in Egypt. God asks Moses to deliver his kinsmen from their plight, to which Moses replies, "Who am I that I should go to Pharaoh, and that I should bring the children of Israel out of Egypt?" (Exod 3:11, KJV)

Notice on whom Moses is focused? Let me paraphrase God's response to Moses: "Why did you bring 'I' into the picture . . . I didn't say you would do it on your own. I'm the One who will bring them out, involving you as my representative. If you cooperate with Me, you will share in *My* glory."

A person who doesn't understand the difference between humiliation and humility might mistake Moses as a very humble servant because of his aw-shucks attitude. But as we read on we realize that Moses had the false sort of humility that is really a cover for pride. We see that Moses argued with God five times from a self-focused perspective. He complains, "I won't know what to say," and "Suppose they will not listen to my voice" (Exod 3:11, 4:1). He builds his case by lamenting, "O my Lord, I am not eloquent" (Exod 4:10). Finally he begs, "Please send someone else" (Exod 4:13). Then God's patience gives out and His call to Moses becomes a command.

Do you see it? Moses was focused on himself and his fear of failure. He had no faith that the sovereign God of the entire universe had sought him out to do a special job. Instead of focusing on what an awesome partnership he was invited to experience with the great "I Am," Moses instead got bound up in himself.

Fortunately, Moses gradually learned to apply the antidote. If you read through the entire case history of his life, you will see how patiently God worked with Moses. Moses was molded into a man of godly humility—probably the most truly humble servant in history, next to Jesus Christ.

Jeremiah

Another man who struggled with the problem of inferiority was the prophet Jeremiah. In fact, in the first chapter of his writings we read about a conversation he had with God that sounds similar to the one God had with Moses in Exodus. God calls Jeremiah to be His prophet, a powerful spokesman to His people, and Jeremiah says, "I do not know how to speak. I'm only a child" (Jer 1:6).

I have my own theory about Jeremiah, Moses, and tens of thousands of others like them who have lived through the ages. One reason they had such a problem with taking their focus off themselves and leaning on God is because they were men and women of such tremendous human ability. Moses is historically regarded as one of the world's most gifted leaders. Jeremiah was part of the intelligent, well-educated priestly class. Both had impressive natural abilities. I know it seems contradictory, but I think their human strengths made them vulnerable to the spiritual toxin of inferiority.

Earlier I mentioned that high-achievers are more prone to low self-esteem. People who are high achievers often have a crippling fear of failure. These are the people who are least likely to fail, but who are most likely to *fear* failure. And fear poisons the soul, weakening faith. Without faith, it is impossible to connect with God and to please Him (Heb 11:6).

Because Jeremiah and Moses were hung up on their own human abilities, they had trouble tapping in to God's superhuman power. God had to train both men—just as He has to train you and me—through hands-on experiences that forced them to submit to His lordship in their lives. Somehow, toxic feelings of insufficiency get lost in God's amazing *all*-sufficiency, and it is through humble dependence on Him that we find a way to escape crippling low self-esteem.

Amos

The Bible gives us another example—this time a man who chose to focus on God from the start, and so was able to avoid some of the struggles of Moses and Jeremiah. The man's name was Amos.

Amos was the kind of fellow that didn't have a lot of natural ability with regard to God's call to be a prophet. He was a simple man, an introvert. He wasn't a "people person," but rather preferred to be off on his own, working with his hands. You might say that Amos lived a simple life that he was comfortable with, because it fit his personality. Nevertheless, God chose him to go to the most sophisticated court in all the land, the palace of mighty King Amaziah, to warn him of God's impending judgment.

As you might imagine, Amos was met with disdain. "Go, you seer!" said the king. "It is the king's sanctuary . . . the royal residence" (Amos 7:13). And when Amos answered, he made it clear that he knew who and what he was and that he didn't particularly want to be there either (Amos 7:14–15).

Amos accepted that he was inadequate, but God had asked him to do something for Him and, without hesitation, he set about doing it, placing his focus on the Lord's adequacy. Unlike Moses and Jeremiah, Amos wasted no time wrestling with feelings of inferiority. He knew the source of success was not himself, but the Lord. So he was able to move boldly forward, to march right up to a powerful king and stand before him as a spokesman for the Living God. If we could only get our hearts around this principle of total reliance on God, as Amos did, we wouldn't have to live with feelings of self-doubt.

Reading about Amos makes me think of a man I talked to once when a family called on me to conduct a funeral service. I had to contact another pastor who would be involved in leading the service along with me, and since I didn't know him, I called directory assistance and got what I thought was the correct phone number. I dialed the number and introduced myself, informing the man that the family had asked me to enlist his help in leading the service for their deceased loved one. There was a long, awkward silence, finally broken by the voice of a gentleman who sounded as though he might be quite elderly: "Son, I've worked my whole life using my hands. I don't know a thing about leading a funeral service." There was terror in his voice, and then I realized I had called the wrong guy.

Biblical Antidotes to Toxic Inferiority

Are you more like Moses and Jeremiah—focused on your own inadequacies? Or can you relate more to Amos, a man who trusted God to make up for his inadequacies? If you are a person who struggles with low self-esteem, perhaps these scriptural case histories will be an encouragement to you. Along with Moses, Jeremiah, Amos, and many other men and women, you are in very good company. As we've seen, the key to conquering our feelings of inadequacy is to focus on the Lord's adequacy.

Psychologist Bill Backus has been called the father of Christian cognitive therapy, an approach he uses as he works with his clients. Cognitive therapy helps individuals to recognize the destructive "self-talk" that goes on in their mind. These are negative messages that employ wrong standards to judge behavior. They learn to replace ungodly thinking with godly thinking, based on principles from God's Word.

This simple practice can be an effective part of a personal treatment plan to combat toxic feelings of inferiority. So let's look now at a few biblical principles that we can employ when crippling negative self-talk starts playing through our mind like an audiocassette.

Principle #1: Make a deliberate choice to acknowledge your importance to God, who mapped out a plan for your life even before your birth.
Ponder these words:

> *Your eyes saw my unformed body.*
> *All the days ordained for me were written in your*
> *book before one of them came to be. (Ps 139:16, NIV)*

What a great assurance of God's personal interest in your life! Before you were ever born, when you were an idea being fashioned in

God's mind, He loved you and planned every single day of your life. If God Almighty thought so much of you even before He created you, then shouldn't you treasure the life He gave you and allow His plans to be realized through you?

Principle #2: Remember that your life is "in process," and that God is still growing you into the person He designed you to be. Paul says, "He who began a good work in you will carry it to completion until the day of Christ Jesus" (Phil 1:6). So relax and remember that all God asks of you is your cooperation.

Sometimes we struggle because we feel we should be instantly complete. When I was in seminary, I heard about a student who was intensely anxious the first time he was called on to help lead a service. All he was asked to do was to lead the congregation in saying the Lord's Prayer—not too tough. But when the time came, he was so nervous that he found himself saying, "Now let us pray together the prayer that our Lord taught us to pray: I pledge allegiance to the flag of the United States of America. . . ."

Most of us have disastrous "firsts" like this that remind us that expertise takes practice. Making mistakes like the one my friend made simply illustrates our need to relax and let God work through us, rather than trying to do things in our own strength.

When God conquered spiritual death at your conversion, He also started a living work in you, and He will personally perform that work through you as you allow Him to.

Principle #3: Refuse to compare yourself with other people. Few things open the door for more unhappiness and disappointment than to hold ourselves up for comparison against another person. No matter how good you are at something, you will always find someone who is a little bit better. So why even start this demoralizing cycle?

When we measure ourselves against others, we always seem to hold up our worst traits against someone else's best traits. We gaze at them through rose-colored glasses that make them look so good that we can't even see their faults. We compare our cooking to the culinary artistry of Julia Childs. We expect our parenting skills to beat those of James and Shirley Dobson. We measure our intelligence against the genius of Albert Einstein. No wonder we develop feelings of inferiority.

Even the apostle Peter fell into this trap when he questioned Jesus about the plans He had for his future in comparison to those He predicted for John. Jesus sternly rebuked Peter, saying, in effect, "It's none of your business, Peter. Just follow Me and yield to my plan for your life and you will be fulfilled" (John 21:22). Jesus' words for Peter—"You must follow Me"—are the same words He has for us today. We must not live our lives constantly begrudging what God has given us. When we try to live the life God has given to somebody else, it opens the door to dissatisfaction and jealousy. It robs us of joy.

Principle #4: To avoid low self-esteem, learn to respond correctly to your shortcomings.

Biblical humility with a grateful dependence on God opens the door for Him to give the abundant life He wants us to have. The apostle Paul, perhaps the greatest servant of Christ in all of history, strove against a chronic "thorn in the flesh" that he felt hindered his ministry. God never removed the thorn, but instead taught Paul to accept it and grow through it, allowing His strength to be perfected through Paul's weakness (2 Corinthians 12).

Accepting—even embracing—our inadequacies gives God the opportunity to be glorified through us and enables us to be at peace with ourselves.

Finding Your Niche

Applying these principles will be easier if we see ourselves as a "vital organ" in the body of Christ—an important partner with Him in performing His mission on earth. We learn from scripture that "we were all baptized by one Spirit into one body" (1 Cor 12:13). We all know that the most vital parts in our physical bodies are the ones that can't be seen. For example, if you were here with me you could see my right ear, my nose, and my left pinkie finger. I could live without any of those parts. But you would not be able to see my heart or my liver, and I couldn't survive without these crucial organs.

This is a great analogy for the body of Christ. Sometimes the most useful people are the ones who work quietly behind the scenes. In God's eyes, there are no useless people. Everyone has a custom-designed niche only he or she can fill.

Have you found your niche? If you have, you already know that life can be lived apart from exhausting self-effort. Every day can be one of joy and fulfillment. And when we are not striving so hard to succeed in our own strength, we have greater self-respect and contentment in Him.

Remember Whose You Are

We've looked at case histories, we've applied some biblical principles, and we've examined scriptures that assure us of our importance to God. It's clear that we don't need to struggle with toxic feelings of inferiority. And yet we know that we will from time to time. So what's the bottom line?

For me it's as simple as this: As the lyrics of the famous hymn played at every Billy Graham crusade proclaim, God loves and accepts me "just as I am." And if God, Who is eternally perfect, can love me, then surely I can learn to at least *like* myself.

Sometimes when I am struggling in this area, I remember that I am "God's workmanship, created in Christ Jesus to do good works" (Eph 2:10). In the original Greek, the word for workmanship means "a work of art."

Did you know that God regards you as a treasured "work of art"? No one like you has preceded you, and no such person will follow you. You are one of a kind. Jesus expressed this beautifully when He said:

> *Look at the birds of the air; they do not sow or reap or store away in barns, and yet your heavenly Father feeds them. Are you not much more valuable than they? (Matt 6:26, NIV)*

A few years ago, I was reading a *Newsweek* article on Dan Quayle. This was at the time when he was under tough personal scrutiny. *Newsweek's* poll revealed that only 43 percent of those asked thought he was competent to perform the role of vice president of the United States. But in the very same article, President Bush was quoted as saying that Dan Quayle was doing a "first-rate" job. The president was Mr. Quayle's boss, and his opinion was really the only one that mattered. The other 250 million people didn't count, when all was said and done.

The same principle applies to you. If the God of the universe says that you have value, then you do. If He says you are a work of art, then you are a masterpiece. You have value in His eyes, regardless of what others think of you, or even of what you think of yourself. You belong to God, bought for the sacred price of His Son's life.

So when those uncomfortable, crippling feelings of toxic inferiority assault you, just remember Whose you are and cling stubbornly to His love. It's a sure-fire antidote for even the most toxic feelings of inferiority.

Applying the Antidote

On a card, write one personal strength and one weakness. Say a prayer and conduct a little test. Thank God for the strength and commit it to His use. Ask God to use the weakness in some way for your good and His glory. Seal the card in an envelope marked with the date that is six months from the day you write the card. Place it in your Bible or somewhere where you will see it often. In six months, evaluate how God has answered your prayer. I bet you'll be surprised.

For: Inferiority

"How precious is it, Lord, to realize that you are thinking about me constantly! I can't even count how many times a day your thoughts turn toward me. And when I waken in the morning, you are still thinking of me!"

—Ps 139:17–18 (TLB)

Chapter 4

Toxic Loneliness

❧

*Then the Lord God said,
"It is not good for the man
to be alone; I will make
him a helper suitable for him."*

—Gen 2:18 (NASB)

❧

In the beginning, even before God designed a human cell, He first prepared the environment, anticipating every possible need.

He placed the sun, moon, planets, and stars in the sky to provide light and order. Oceans, mountains, animals of all kinds, flowers, and foliage—God designed all these wonders to delight and support the creature who would be made in His image to reign over all creation: man. After man was finally fashioned—after He named him Adam and presented him with all the gifts He had custom-made—God stepped back. He took a look and saw that His human child was desperately lonely. So He created the first woman to fill the yearning in Adam's heart.

Loneliness is one of the most basic human emotions. It's also one of the most painful experiences we endure. Throughout our lives it touches every one of us, at least to some degree.

Adam's story illustrates that God is concerned about our need for companionship and fellowship. Yet He permits loneliness. Why? Because He wants us to draw nearer to Him, and sometimes He has to allow us to feel isolated and alone in order to make us aware of our hunger for His companionship.

God also uses loneliness to loosen the hold of earthly ties and to make our hearts ready to let go of this place when the time comes for us to die. I have seen God use loneliness, over and over, to teach and to stretch His people.

Causes of Loneliness

There are many causes of loneliness. A broken relationship or the death of a loved one leaves us feeling alone, even though we may be surrounded by people every day. The elderly often face intense loneliness in the "winter" season of their lives when retirement, spousal death, or the exit of their children suddenly cut them off from those they love and enjoy most. And anyone who has ever moved from one place to another knows the lonely feeling of being a stranger in a foreign city, far from everything that is familiar and comfortable.

Some people are constantly surrounded by others, and yet they feel lonely. Why? Because "quantity" is not as important as "quality." When so many people are around on a regular basis, relationships can tend to be shallow and unsatisfying. Even when you're involved with many people every day, it's sometimes difficult to get close. This type of loneliness—emotional isolation—is one of the most frustrating and painful. It's like suffering from terrible thirst while being surrounded by the ocean or a sea. Water is all around, but it's not fit for drinking and it can't satisfy our thirst.

Like an Owl among the Ruins: The Psalmist's Cry

Scriptural offers plenty of examples of people suffering from loneliness. Sometimes I think we have a mistaken notion that the men and women of biblical times were super-spiritual, having such a close walk with God that they were never prone to human struggles as we are. Nothing could be further from the truth. As a matter of fact, God's Word indicates that those who are most intimate with the Lord often go through seasons of loneliness and depression.

Psalm 102 is the testimony of such a person. Listen to the psalmist's lament:

> *Hear my prayer, O Lord; let my cry for help come to you. Do not hide your face from me when I am in distress. Turn your ear to me; when I call, answer me quickly. For my days vanish like smoke; my bones burn like glowing embers. My heart is blighted and withered like grass; I forget to eat my food. Because of my loud groaning I am reduced to skin and bones. I am like a desert owl, like an owl among the ruins. (Ps 102:1–6, NIV)*

Have you ever heard the plaintive call of an owl, interrupting the silence of a dark night? It's a very lonely sound.

Imagine a desert ghost town—empty, falling into ruin. The only living thing remaining in this place, once bustling with life, is a solitary owl. To me, this is a very graphic portrait of the utter devastation of loneliness.

Our Comrade in Loneliness: Jesus Christ

The next time you feel lonely, maybe it will help you to remember that you are traveling in good company. Many biblical personalities suffered from loneliness, including our Savior himself.

One of the loneliest moments in all of history is recorded in Matthew 26, beginning in verse 30. It's the night before Jesus was crucified, and we find Him in the Garden of Gethsemane, wrestling with His heavenly Father over the destiny He was about to fulfill. I can only imagine His agony. Sometimes, because we know He is God, we forget that Jesus was also a man and subject to all the struggles and emotions that we wrestle with.

Facing the cross to rescue us from eternity in hell was no easy task for Jesus. That night, He needed His friends around Him, supporting and encouraging Him, praying for Him and with Him. Instead, they fell asleep. Jesus was abandoned by His closest friends at the darkest hour of His life. All alone, He knelt and cried out to God, "Take away this cup."

But as lonely as that night was, there was a still lonelier time to come for Jesus.

The Ninth Hour

Without a doubt, the loneliest time in Christ's life—and in all of recorded history—was when He hung on a cross, stripped and beaten, humiliated and suffering. No one came to rescue Him, though He was there for the sake of every man, woman, and child who stood and watched Him die.

And then there was that agonizing moment that is hard for us to fathom, that instant when even God turned away. Jesus was left to suffer and die alone.

The way that felt is something we can't possibly relate to because every one of us, whether we have committed our hearts to Christ or not, enjoys what is called "common grace." Though we may not acknowledge His existence, God's presence is nevertheless all around us in this world. None of us has ever been totally separated from God.

But Jesus was. He hung on the cross from the sixth to the ninth hour. As He endured the most intense suffering imaginable, darkness moved in as if to swallow Him. Think of His terror as He cried out to His Father, "My God, my God, why have you forsaken me?"

But there was no answer. In one terrifying moment of utter loneliness and rejection, Jesus paid the costly price for our sins. Alone. For me—for all of us—the most horrible part of being in hell would be the utter desolation that comes from God's absence. I am so grateful that Jesus loved me enough—and loved you enough—to experience hell for our sake, even though He was the only person who ever lived who did not deserve this judgment.

The Apostle Paul

Loneliness is at least a little less unbearable when I remember that Jesus knows how it feels. I'm sure that was also a comfort to the apostle Paul, who endured some pretty lonely moments during his ministry. Let's take a look at some of those moments and see what practical help we can learn from Paul's experiences.

If you have studied Paul's life, you know that he was not the kind of guy you would expect to be susceptible to loneliness. He was an extroverted, outgoing, "do-er" kind of man. But in the New Testament, we have an account of a very lonely time in Paul's life (2 Timothy 4). There were five reasons for Paul's loneliness during this time.

A Lonely Cell

The first was his environment—a lonely prison cell, far away from everyone he loved. Paul had been imprisoned before, but it was a "house arrest" and it was not that uncomfortable for him. Although he was not free to leave the premises, he was able to visit with friends and continue with his ministry. Although he was confined, he was not isolated from other people or from the activities and responsibilities he was committed to. But here he was locked away, all by himself.

Depression

Depression was a second factor that enhanced Paul's loneliness. During this second incarceration, he was in a place called the Mammertine Prison, in Rome.

I had occasion to visit this prison once, and it is still a very depressing place—cold, dark, bleak, and uncomfortable. I was certainly glad that I was only a tourist, and not one of the many poor souls who had spent time locked up in Mammertine Prison. But Paul was one of those prisoners, and when he was there it was winter, a gloomy time of year. Psychologists say winter is the season when we are most susceptible to depression.

Paul was also experiencing another type of "season"—a time when his ministry was winding down and the end was in sight. Normally, Paul was active, busy, always on the move. But here in prison, it was as if he had been put on the shelf, like a setup for loneliness.

Have you ever felt that you've been filed away? You've been involved and active, busy and productive, and suddenly, for a period of time, it feels as though God has set you aside. You feel useless and lonely. This is often the way people feel when they first enter into retirement. Some experience intense loneliness during this, or any, transitional time.

The Last Lap

Paul often used the analogy of "running the race" to describe his ministry. Here, in this scene, we see a third reason for Paul's loneliness: His work on earth was coming to an end. The finish line was in sight.

Paul affirms his awareness of this when he says, "I am already being poured out like a drink offering, and the time has come for my departure" (2 Tim 4:6). Paul sensed that he did not have much longer to live, and even though he knew he would soon be in God's house, he needed the support and encouragement of other human beings to walk through that door into the Kingdom.

As Christians, we sometimes feel like spiritual failures if we struggle with loneliness and depression as we approach illness or death. This is an area where the church needs to work hard at being sensitive and supportive. God created millions and billions of people, not just one. He expects us to be there for each other during times of trial, when we are facing the unknown.

When the Chips Are Down

This brings us to the fourth reason why Paul was suffering from loneliness: When the chips were down for him, the people he needed around him most were not there. We learn that "Demas, in love with this present world," deserted Paul and moved to Thessolonica (2 Tim 4:10). Two other friends, Crescens and Titus, also departed to other locations. Paul knew that he was a partner in ministry with these men, and I'm sure he understood that the work needed to continue. But that did not diminish the loneliness he felt as a result of their leaving him alone in prison. We sense how hurt he was feeling when he writes that "no one came to my support, but everyone deserted me" (2 Tim 4:16).

Under Scrutiny

A final reason for Paul's loneliness was that he was under scrutiny by such critics as "Alexander the metal worker" (2 Tim 4:14), who was opposed to Christianity and seized Paul's hardship as an occasion to taunt him and make an example of him to onlookers. What a lonely, discouraging experience this must have been.

In prison . . . nearing the end of his life . . . under attack . . . friendless. How did Paul cope with this loneliest moment in his life? What practical help we can glean by taking a look at his example.

It's a Choice to Rejoice

Paul had a choice, and it is the same choice that you and I have whenever we face loneliness. When our friends and loved ones have disappointed us, we can either give in to self-pity and bitterness, or we can take concrete, proactive steps to reject the bitterness and disappointment and turn to Jesus, the one trustworthy Friend who will never forsake us. We can press hard into Him, rejoicing in the strength and comfort of His presence in and around us.

This was the choice Paul made, and Jesus showed him five concrete steps to deal with the "toxic loneliness" that was threatening to keep him from finishing his race triumphantly.

Choice #1: Heavenly Mindedness

The first step Paul took was to consciously choose to put his mind on Christ and the eternal inheritance he was about to receive. Here's what he said:

> I have fought the good fight, I have finished the race, I have kept the faith. Now there is in store for me the crown of righteousness, which the Lord, the righteous Judge, will award to me on that day. (2 Tim 4:7–8, NIV)

Paul chose to divert his focus from his brief moment of loneliness to the imminent and infinite companionship he would soon enjoy with his best friend, Jesus Christ. I'll bet he closed his eyes as he huddled in that cell and tried to imagine what that divine face would look like. Perhaps he even envisioned himself as a hurting little boy who runs to the strong arms of his father. Nestled there, how could he feel lonely or alone?

You see, Paul knew what the final outcome was going to be. He had experienced God's trustworthiness, and he had been assured that Christ would be the ultimate victor. As Paul turned his thoughts toward Jesus, he was comforted and sustained. Victory was a sure thing.

I like to tease my wife, Kimberly, about her faithful determination not to miss her favorite television program, *Rescue 911.* If you've ever watched this show, you've probably noticed a pattern. Someone gets into trouble, then they get out of trouble—like cause and effect. Sometimes I goad her a little bit about watching a show over and over when the outcome is so predictable. But the fact is, it's comforting to be able to know the outcome, especially when it means that good triumphs over evil. It's reassuring to have reminders that it's all going to work out fine in the end. And since God has given us reminders in the Bible, let's go to them regularly to draw comfort from His promises that our lonely lives will ultimately end in a happy union with Him.

Choice #2: Seeking Help from Others
Sometimes it's hard to shake our feelings of loneliness all on our own. We are, after all, human beings. We are not all-sufficient all the time. So the second thing Paul did was to choose to seek help from others—from people he had previously helped. And because Paul had been there for these people, they were, in turn, there for him at the time of his need. There's a lesson to be heeded here. Most of the time we can count on help from others if we have been there for them when they have needed help from us. It's the "I'll scratch your back if you'll scratch mine" principle. It's not a matter of doing things for others with ulterior motives. In this case, it's an illustration of the biblical principle that God created us to "bear one another's burdens." It's a two-way street, and that's the way it ought to be. But sometimes we have to ask for help, as in Paul's case.

We've already seen that some of Paul's teammates in ministry had gone off and left him alone. Look at how Paul asks Timothy to round up some friends:

Do your best to come to me quickly. . . . Only Luke is with me.
Get Mark and bring him with you, because he is helpful to me
in my ministry. Do your best to get here before winter. (2 Tim 4:
9–11, 21, NIV)

Can you hear the almost urgent pleading that underlies his re-
quest for support? In that plea, Paul makes himself vulnerable, and
that's pretty hard for many of us to do. Often we play a game with
our friends and loved ones. For some reason, we don't feel we have
the right to just ask for their help. We expect them to read our mind,
know our hurts, and take the first step to reach out and to help meet
our needs. And if they don't, we feel bruised and hurt by what we
perceive to be their insensitivity.

Games like this can be a setup for hurt feelings and grudges
that will damage our most important relationships. Paul shows us
an example here of what we should do instead. We need to risk being vulnerable and even to humble ourselves, if necessary, in order
to get help from others when we need it. If we don't ask for help
from others, they might miss out on the privilege of ministering in
a situation where God wants to use them as ambassadors of His
comfort.

Asking for help is particularly hard for a capable person who is
used to being in control. Paul was like that: comfortable with others
leaning on him, a leader who took charge. But even Paul had times in
his life when he needed the help of others. So do we. The next time
this happens in your life, imitate Paul. There's no shame in asking
for help.

Choice #3: Responsible Self-Care

A third choice Paul made was taking care of his physical needs. During times of loneliness, it's common to neglect our bodies, minds,
and souls. We don't eat right, we get inadequate sleep, we become
"couch potatoes." We have no desire to attend to our need for food,

sleep, or activity, even though attending to those needs is exactly what is needed to shake the feelings of loneliness and depression.

We also tend to fill our minds with negative thoughts, to become hypnotized by television and videos, or to escape into a good suspense novel. Although there is nothing inherently wrong with any of these activities (except negative thinking), we have to be careful not to use them as escape mechanisms that keep us from taking the practical steps God wants us to take in order to get past our loneliness.

Choice #4: Reaching Outward

When we are lonely, we tend to become self-focused and self-centered, a deadly combination. Have you ever noticed how much better you feel if you get your mind off your problems and onto someone else's? When we reach out to help someone else who is hurting—when we encourage others—the returns come back at us. We feel better. Paul knew this and so, a fourth choice Paul made was to take the focus off himself and to put it on other people. He certainly had every reason to turn inward and be absorbed in his own problems, but instead Paul was always thinking of his "flock." He called for his parchment scrolls and wrote letters to encourage and strengthen others. Even from his prison cell he sent greetings to such friends as Priscilla and Aquila, and prayed diligently for them (see 2 Tim: 19, 21, 22).

And as Paul concentrated on encouraging others, gradually he was encouraged—and discouragement began to ebb.

Choice #5: What a Friend!

Finally, Paul always held close the assurance that Jesus was his best friend—the Friend Who would never leave him, even in his darkest hour.

We can count on several things when we are going through tough times. First, our enemies to be consistent. They will predictably pour salt on our wounds and drag us down as far as they can.

We can also count on our friends to be inconsistent. Because of human frailty, on occasion our friends will fail us—very likely at a time when we need them the most. Our church family will fail us, as will our pastor and our family. It won't be intentional, but because we are imperfect, it will happen. Count on it.

But there is one person we can count on to always be there for us. The Bible tells us that there is a friend who sticks closer to us than a brother, a friend who never wants us to be lonely (Prov 18:24). That friend is our Savior.

A young man in Africa was undergoing a tribal rite of initiation into manhood. In his culture, it was customary to spend the night alone in the jungle, so the young initiate stationed himself outdoors to keep vigil through the night. Barely more than a boy, fear gripped him as the sun set. Chills went up his spine as he listened to the threatening noises of animals and other jungle sounds.

To deal with the terror, the youth began to sing, "Come by here, Lord. Come by here." Throughout the long, dark, and lonely night the boy drew strength from his song. As the sun rose the next morning, the boy proudly breathed a sigh of relief for making it through the ordeal. Then he turned and saw his own father standing about a hundred feet away with a spear in one hand and a bow and arrow in the other. He laughed as he realized he hadn't needed to be afraid; his father had been close by, watching over him.

What a picture this story paints of our own position in Christ. We may go through periods of deep darkness in this world. We may sometimes feel as if we are isolated, even from God. But our heavenly Father is always close by, always in control.

"For Thou Art with Me"

Remember the verse in Psalm 23 that says, "Even though I walk through the valley of the shadow of death, I will fear no evil, for You (God) are with me"?

Do you experience this kind of confidence even in your loneliest, most difficult moments? When you have physical or financial problems, do you cling to God's closeness? When your deepest relationships break down, do you draw comfort from the knowledge that He is still with you?

Paul did. He affirms that "the Lord stood at my side and gave me strength, so that through me His message might be fully proclaimed, and all the Gentiles might hear it" (2 Tim 4:17). As Paul went through the greatest trial of his life, he looked in one direction and saw his enemies, gloating over his situation. He looked the other way and saw that his friends had failed him. But it didn't really matter, because Jesus stood by his side through every lonely moment.

The Antidote

Loneliness. It can be toxic, but it doesn't have to be. With His Word to uphold us, His Spirit to fill us, and His Son to save us, our Heavenly Father has provided the antidote that ensures our eternal companionship with Him—a never-ending supply of it. With a friend like Jesus by your side, you never have to be lonely again.

Applying the Antidote

Choose a comfortable, quiet place—perhaps a soft chair or sofa. Sit or recline there and close your eyes. Paint a mental picture of yourself with your best friend, Jesus. In the scene, it's just the two of you; you have the undivided attention of the King of kings. Think of the look of pure pleasure on His face as He enjoys being with you. Use this mental scene as a tool to draw near to Him whenever you feel an onset of toxic loneliness. Apply it as a reminder that you are never really alone, and that you never need to be lonely with Jesus nearby.

For: Loneliness

"And surely I am with you always, to the very end of the age."

—MATT 28:20 (NIV)

Toxic Anger

IMAGINE THAT YOU'RE sitting in a fast-food restaurant, enjoying your favorite junk food, when you become aware of a family in the booth next to you. From all outward appearance they look like a typical American family.

What causes you to notice them is the following scene, played out before your eyes.

Act 1, Scene 1

Two-year-old boy (spills milk):

Mother (gasps, harshly slaps little hand, and speaks in a loud voice): Look what you've done, Joey! You spilled your milk all over the place. You're a very bad boy.

Toddler (begins to cry)

Father (calmly looks at mother): He just spilled his milk. Stop crying, Joey.

You watch as an angry mother jerks her pouting baby out of high chair and heads to the car, followed by the cool, calm, self-righteous dad. You feel embarrassment for the angry mom, tender protection toward the toddler, and admiration for the easy-going dad. That is, until you glance through the window and see him having a hard time getting the car to start.

Act 1, Scene 2

(Sound of car grinding, won't start.)

Father (once-calm face turns purple and distorted):
   [Expletives deleted!]

When was the last time you got irrationally angry? Personally, I wish I could say that it's been a long, long time. But the truth is, I often get angry and lose control. There are triggers that set me off before I can catch myself.

What makes you angry? If you look again carefully at the opening mini-drama, you might notice that the mother got angry with a person: her boy. But the father didn't lose it until he had a problem with an object: his car.

Did you know that women tend to get angrier with other people, while men are more prone to explode at gadgets, objects, and machinery? Maybe this doesn't jibe with your own anger tendencies, but it's right-on for me: I go crazy at the mere thought of opening the hood of my car to deal with a mechanical problem.

Psychologists identify five distinct stages of anger development, ranging from mildly annoyed to dangerously out of control. Like a thermometer, when the heat is on the mercury keeps on rising. If we don't learn how to control our anger in the beginning stages, it will eventually escalate and take control of us.

The Five Stages of Anger

Initially, anger takes the form of mild irritation, a feeling of discomfort triggered by a person, an event, or perhaps a circumstance. Most of us experience irritation on an everyday basis; it's a fact of life. But if we don't deal with irritation, it can escalate to the second level of anger, which is indignation. Irritation feeds on frustration, especially when we perceive something to be unfair or unreasonable, and that's when indignation takes over.

A third stage of anger is wrath. This is when irritation and indignation grow stronger in intensity. In this state, we have an impulse to avenge or punish. It's impossible to repress and can come out in a number of ways that are all unpleasant. And when wrath heats up, it reaches the fourth stage, which is violent fury and a temporary loss of control.

Anger has reached the fifth, and most dangerous, stage when it turns to rage. The outcome of rage is often tragic, ending with people getting hurt—perhaps even killed. The really disturbing factor is that people who are enraged usually are so out of control that they are unaware of what they are doing until it is too late to stop.

As Christians, we are obviously nervous about anger. Because we represent Jesus, we have a responsibility to reflect His character. If anger takes control of us, people look on with disgust and sometimes unjustly make judgments about Jesus Christ based on our sinful behavior. We also fear anger because we don't want to lose control in ways that might get us into trouble.

Yes, it's good to have a healthy reticence about getting angry. But it's not good to suppress our feelings of irritation and indignation or to pretend that our anger does not exist. All we have to do is watch the morning news to know that the consequences of suppressing anger can be devastating. It's going to come out—that's a given—either in acts of aggression toward others or turned inward on ourselves. Depression and illness, both physical and psychological, are a few of the consequences people reap from "stuffing" their anger.

Sometimes we deal with anger by being passive-aggressive. We drag our feet when asked to do something, or simply treat others with coolness. Christians seem particularly prone to this frustrating behavior, since we are conditioned to believe that it is wrong to be overtly angry. So instead we take our anger out on people in other ways.

This style of expression can be maddening. A much better approach is to openly acknowledge our anger to ourselves and to God, who can help us bring it under control.

The Bible speaks a lot about the issue of self-control. For example, we are commanded not to hate, regardless of the situation we are in. But we also learn that it is not a sin to feel angry.

In other words, it's not bad to have anger. However, it is bad to respond incorrectly to it. We must learn to control it. We are going to look at some antidotes from God's Word that will help us in that pursuit.

Anger without Sin

How do we get angry without sinning? A key is to realize that anger is an emotion, and all of our emotions are gifts from God. Therefore, there is a positive way to look at anger. In fact, we can even go so far as to thank God for our anger, though many of us would never think of doing that. You see, anger can produce a good result, if we respond correctly to it.

What would happen in this world if no one ever got angry. There would be no constructive response to social injustices. There would be no motivation to take steps to change things in our life. There would be no righteous discipline of children when they misbehave. There would be no change, no growth. Things would remain stagnant.

The Bible clearly teaches that anger is not always wrong. There are eighteen instances spoken of in the Old Testament where God got angry. And in the New Testament, we are told of a time when Jesus became so angry over the dishonest dealings of money-changers in the temple that He drove them outside. Since God and Jesus cannot sin, then these records indicate that anger in and of itself is not sinful. Even so, let's not jump to the conclusion that we should just let our anger rip

Paul cautions us, "In your anger, do not sin" (Eph 4:26). He says we are not to sin in response to our anger. And he goes onto say, "Do not let the sun go down while you are still angry" (Eph 4:27).

This verse identifies several "fences" we should build around our anger. First, we must impose a limited duration of time on anger. We must deal with it, so that it doesn't feed on itself and keep going and going—and growing.

Second, we must impose a limited depth on our anger. As Paul says, "do not give the devil a foothold" (Eph 4:27). If we allow anger to put down roots deep inside us, Satan will surely make them hard to pull up. He will stir us deeper and deeper into a downward spiral, until once-righteous anger turns toxic. When that happens, we are in trouble.

Directing Our Anger

How can we ensure that our anger remains "righteous"? I think we would agree that this is one of the great, enduring challenges of all time. God's Word holds the answer to that question. Consider these scriptural models of nontoxic anger.

One good example is found in Exodus 32. Here we see that anger is constructive and appropriate in instances where someone is breaking God's rules. Let me recap the scene.

Moses is the key player—and Moses was a man who had a big problem with his temper. In fact, before he yielded control of his life to God, Moses once killed a man in a fit of rage. But when God began to work on him, Moses began to be angry about the right things.

In Exodus 32, we see that Moses had just received the Ten Commandments from God. He had left the children of Israel alone for a short time while he went with the Lord to be instructed with these laws that would protect and structure the Israelites' lives in health and righteousness. He returned to the camp, and to his horror he saw that the people were worshiping a golden calf—an idol. The people knew only God was worthy of worship, and that He had forbidden the worship of idols. Yet left alone for a short time they fell into this terrible sin. And that made Moses mad.

I hope we have videotapes in heaven because the next scene is one I want to see: When Moses reentered the camp, he did some pretty extreme things. He was so angry that he took the calf they had made and he burned it. Then he ground it to powder, scattered it on the water, and made the Israelites drink it.

But he was angry about the right thing. When you've been entrusted to lead God's people and they choose to rebel against God, you have a legitimate reason to become angry.

Another example of nontoxic, righteous anger is found in 1 Samuel 11. We read that an Israelite city was besieged and surrounded by Ammonites, under the leadership of a man named Nahash. Nahash gave the Israelites an unpleasant ultimatum: Surrender or be killed. The trouble was, even if they surrendered, every Jewish man, woman, and child would have their right eye gouged out. They managed to buy seven days time from the enemy, and during that time Saul heard of their plight. When he heard of this outrageous threat against his people, he was furious. Scripture tells that the Holy Spirit kindled his anger: "When Saul heard their words, the spirit of God came upon him in power, and he burned with anger" (1 Sam 11:6).

God's enemies were moving into His territory, and so He actually planted anger in Saul in order to move him to come to their defense. As a result, the enemy was defeated. In a similar way, God sometimes plants anger in our hearts when Satan moves into our territory. Perhaps the threat comes from drugs or alcohol that place a child or loved one in jeopardy. Or maybe Satan places discontent in the heart of one spouse, hoping to destroy a godly marriage. In these cases, it's all right to feel angry.

A while back, I attended a reunion of my college class. If you have ever gone to one of these events, I'm sure you'll agree that it can be a bittersweet experience. It's such fun to see people again and to hear some of the wonderful ways God has worked in their lives. But inevitably there are also tough pills to swallow.

At this particular reunion, I learned that one of my closest friends—a guy who really loved and served the Lord in college—had tried to take his own life. Another pal of mine, a girl who had always been fun-loving and full of life, was unable to attend the reunion because she was in a hospital bed, dying of cancer. When such things happen, my initial reaction is to grieve. But then I get angry, and I want to shake my fist at Satan and say, "You have no business interfering with God's people. I'm angry that you're injuring relationships, breaking hearts, and causing tragedy. You're crossing the boundaries into God's territory."

I think that as Christians, anger is an appropriate reaction when the enemy moves onto our turf.

When Anger Becomes Toxic

As we all know, anger is not always acceptable. Just as often it can be "toxic." When anger stems from a bad motive, it is not justifiable. We can see this in the story of the prodigal son, recorded in Luke 15: 11–32.

When the son returned home, his father welcomed him with open, gracious arms. But the older brother lurked in the wings, full of resentment and jealousy. He felt justified because he was the good kid who always toed the mark for his dad, and his father's unconditional love for the brother who messed up hurt him. His motive was one of deep jealousy. It had great potential for destructive consequences.

Another biblical personality who got angry for the wrong reasons was Jonah, the most successful evangelist in all of recorded history. Not even Billy Graham has had comparable results in turning a whole nation of people away from sin and toward God.

Yet it was Jonah's success for the Lord that made him angry. He was disgusted with the very people he went to rescue; he wanted them to be punished. God did not deal with them according to Jonah's personal agenda. And when Jonah didn't get his own way, he got angry. That kind of anger is toxic.

Finally, there is the trap that most of us fall into on a fairly regular basis. When we react impulsively—rather than thinking before we act—there can be disastrous results. In Eccl 7:9, we read a stern warning: "Do not be quickly provoked in your spirit, for anger resides in the lap of fools." James seconds the warning when he says, "everyone should be quick to listen, slow to speak, and slow to become angry, for man's anger does not bring about the righteous life that God desires" (Jas 1:19–20).

What's a Body to Do?

I think it is wise to issue a word of caution at this point in our study on anger. It can be easy to fall into a trap of imputing right motives to wrong actions, so we must always be careful to stop, think about our anger, and ask ourselves if it is nontoxic or toxic. Otherwise our reaction to it could have tragic results. This can be rather tricky, since sometimes there is a fine line of difference between justifiable and forbidden anger.

We've looked at some examples of nontoxic and toxic anger, and now we're faced with a dilemma: How do we know the difference?

Through the years, many people have come up with different approaches for dealing with anger. Thomas Jefferson, for example, made the suggestion, "When angry, count to ten before you speak; if you are very angry, count to one hundred." Almost a century later, Mark Twain changed that a little and said, "When you are angry, count to four; if you are very angry, swear." Not a very practical—or biblical—solution.

In order to really resolve our anger on a deep level, we must look into God's Word for guidance. And remember, God also empowers us through the Holy Spirit. We are not left alone to follow His guidance. We have an "inside Helper" to direct our efforts and to keep us from denying our anger or venting it in an unhealthy way. With His help, we can process it and move on.

Keeping those facts in mind, let's take a look at five powerful preventatives to keep anger under control in our lives.

Preventative #1: Choose Battles Wisely

In Prov 19:11, we are told that "A man's wisdom gives him patience, it is to his glory to overlook offense." The first preventative measure we can take is to practice choosing the battles we fight. In other words, learn to ignore minor irritations. This may take some practice in the society and culture we dwell in, because we are bombarded with permissive messages to "watch out for good old number one."

One way to apply this preventative is to realize that fighting over things that really don't matter ends up hurting us most. It robs us of time and energy that could be devoted to constructive pursuits. It is to our glory to overlook an offense (Prov 19:11).

Every time we make a choice to yield in a minor dispute, God smiles at us. Remember, Jesus taught that the peacemaker will be blessed (Matt 5:9). At the same time, our behavior in these types of circumstances yields credibility to our Savior and brings glory to God.

Preventative #2: Choose Companions Wisely

Another warning from the book of Proverbs says, "Do not make friends with a hot-tempered man. Do not associate with one easily angered, or you may learn his ways and get yourself ensnared" (Prov 22:24–25).

Have you ever noticed how contagious anger is? I certainly have. There are certain things that I could care less about until someone gets me pumped up over it. Then I find myself spouting off.

Perhaps you're muttering a bit over this one, because sometimes we are forced to spend time with people who are prone to anger. We may have a boss, a spouse, or a parent who pops their cork on a regular basis, and removing yourself from that person is just not an option. But in this case we can build a support structure around us through the cultivation of relationships with several key persons who will help us stay in control when we must spend time with an angry person.

Another type of anger we can "catch" from someone else is the "third-party offense." Have you ever had a person come to you and say they are angry at someone else? This can happen, for example, when a child has a fight with a friend, or perhaps when a spouse is having a hard time with a supervisor at work. As you listen to their story, you find yourself taking on that anger. You know in your head that the problem exists between two other people, but your heart becomes emotionally involved, and pretty soon the other person's anger is inside you. Listening with a sympathetic ear is not the same thing as assuming someone's feelings.

In all of the above cases, discernment is the key. Choose companions—and issues—wisely.

Preventative #3: Zip Your Lip

Another preventative we can apply is to practice silence. In my experience as a pastor, I've observed two basic types of people. The first type is the person whose mind freezes when anger sets in. I fall into this category myself. My mind simply goes blank when I get angry.

In a way this is a real blessing, because while I'm struggling inside, I just can't think of a thing to say.

But there's another type of person who reacts in the opposite way. Anger seems to sharpen their mind—and, unfortunately, their tongue. If you are this type of person, it would be a good idea to memorize Prov 15:1, which says that "A gentle answer turns away wrath, but a harsh word stirs up anger." It isn't wise to speak when we first become angry, because usually the words that come out of the mouth are sharp, harsh, and hurtful. If we wait awhile—count to ten, as Thomas Jefferson suggested—we can begin to gain control of our emotions. Then when we do speak, we will also be in control of our tongue.

Once again, this is easier said than done in a society that encourages self-expression. "Get your feelings out," we are told. And so we do, and often with very sad results. When we do not discipline our tongues, we can inflict deep scars that remain in people's hearts long after the outward reaction fades away. Even if we apologize later, the damage may be done. We may lose the respect, trust, and confidence of someone we dearly love if we are not careful to bridle our temperamental tongues.

Preventative #4: Honesty Is the Best Policy

Perhaps the most important preventative of all, especially for Christians, is to cultivate honesty as we build relationships. If we are gently and kindly open and honest with people as a part of our everyday relationship dynamics, then anger will not build up inside of us—or others.

Sadly, this is an area where the church body falls short. Somehow people seem to think that the most "spiritual" people are those who keep things to themselves and never share their feelings.

Prov 27:6 says, "Wounds from a friend can be trusted, but an enemy multiplies kisses." In other words, a few straight words from a friend offered in a gentle manner are worth thousands of compliments from a two-faced enemy.

Again, people seem to fall into two groups—those who find it easy to share their feelings, and those who don't. For years, I firmly believed that it was more noble and spiritual to hold hurts inside, but God has gradually revealed to me that this is not true. True relationship-builders care enough to share their feelings—to confront hurts head-on so that healing can take place. In fact, that when we deny something is wrong, it has a long-term damaging effect on a relationship.

Perhaps you've heard the body of Christ compared to a bunch of porcupines on a cold winter night. We try to warm up and get close to each other, but in the process we stick each other with our quills. What a great illustration, because each one of us—Christian or not—has a sin nature: quills. We have the right intentions but the wrong style of delivery, and so our words are like painful, sharp barbs.

The only way to build healthy relationships is to openly acknowledge when our quills have stuck. That way, we can work with one another to unmesh them, and a positive, edifying result can take place. Otherwise, we will simply tear apart from one another, and the barbs will leave deep wounds.

When I was a youngster, I recognized early on that there were two very different sides to our extended family. My dad's side, the Gundersons, were the staid Swedes who rarely, if ever, demonstrated any emotion. You might meet an uncle you hadn't seen for fifteen years, and he would simply give you a handshake.

My mother's side of the family, the Nixons, were the opposite. They were more open and vocal about their feelings. "Get it out and get it over with"—that was their motto.

Over time, I gradually concluded that it was preferable to lean more toward the "Nixon style" of family quibbling. There's something very healthy, even liberating, about knowing just where you stand with another person.

A word of caution is called for here. Although I am proposing that being open and honest is healthy, honesty is not the same as brutality. Whenever we confront our anger toward another person, we need to filter it through the Holy Spirit. Remember that we are living witnesses for Jesus Christ, and our ultimate purpose in all things is to love Him, to love ourselves, and to love other people. Honesty needs to be presented in a helpful, edifying way, not as a weapon for attacking another person.

Preventative #5: Take Control

Finally, to avoid devastating results from anger, take control of it. Be forewarned by Prov 25:28: "Like a city whose walls are broken down is a man who lacks self-control." But the good news is that Jesus has given us His Spirit to walk with us through life. We don't have to have "broken walls" if we draw upon His power and strength.

One Man's Story

Dan and Patty clasped each other's hands as they told their amazing story at church one Sunday morning. By the time they were through, men and women alike were grabbing for their handkerchiefs with tear-filled eyes.

Dan began by confessing that he had turned his back on God for half his life. It all began when he was a teenager and his sister, only nineteen-years-old, died in a tragic parachute accident. Dan was a teenager at the time, and to deal with his deep grief he surrounded himself with friends.

On Friday nights, Dan and his friends would gather to drink and party. One evening, they were confronted by a gang. Shots were fired, and a bullet hit a sixteen-year-old buddy who was standing right next to Dan, who cradled him in his arms as he died. Afterward, he was consumed with rage—so much so that a week later he waited in an alley for the man he thought had fired the deadly shot, jumped him, and beat him severely.

Three days later Dan heard that the young man was paralyzed from the waist down. Filled with shame and grief, he broke down and cried and determined never to return to that neighborhood again. Two deeply painful losses and one impulsive act left Dan filled with anger at God. He deliberately turned away from God and devoted himself to putting the past behind him and living his life. From all outward appearances, it seemed as if Dan had been successful. He finished school, got a good job, bought a home, got married, and had two beautiful children. He sank himself into the business of living a "normal life" and stuffed his memories as deep as he possibly could. Dan seemed healthy and well adjusted on the outside, but anger was poisoning his soul—robbing him of the fellowship with God that could satisfy and complete him.

Then one day Patty announced that she and the children were going to church. She invited Dan to come, but he declined. He didn't feel so angry anymore. Now he just felt terribly unworthy. As the weeks went by, Dan became more and more downhearted. On one particularly bad morning, his four-year-old daughter, Emily, drew close to him and said, "It's okay Daddy. If you believe in Jesus and ask Him for help, He'll help you."

Through the words of his own little girl, Dan heard God calling out to him to "come and be healed." After Emily left the room Dan dropped to his knees, tearfully poured out his heart, and followed his daughter's advice. He asked Jesus for help.

There's more to Dan's incredible story. Shortly after this experience, he returned to the neighborhood he had not visited for years and found the man he had beaten. He went to him and begged forgiveness and was astounded when the man said, "I will forgive you, and God forgives you. He led us here today to forgive and forget. He is in your heart or you would not have come here today. Go now, because we are not the devil's workers anymore. We are God's children."

Dan left, but he wasn't satisfied. Unable to forgive himself for taking away that man's legs, he returned again the next day and shared his torment. To his amazement, the man assured him that his paralysis was not from Dan's attack, but rather from a gunshot wound he inflicted on himself after Dan walked away. Depressed over his own life, the former gang member had been intent on killing himself that night—even before the back-alley encounter with Dan.

Set free. That's how Dan felt, and soon afterward he surrendered his life to Jesus Christ. Toxic anger had separated him from God for more than half of his life, but from that moment on Dan would always know where to go for healing. Through Christ's gracious forgiveness, he was cleansed from toxic anger and guilt.

A Final Word of Encouragement

If you are a person who struggles to overcome anger, I want to leave you with a thought from Prov 16:32: "Better a patient man than a warrior, a man who controls his temper than one who takes a city." Don't give up. Be patient and put your sights on a much bigger goal than the moment at hand.

As God works with you to "cure" your anger, He will develop in you the qualities of patience and self-control. This very struggle can eventually turn out to be a way God uses you as a witness. In fact, one of the most powerful statements you can make for Jesus Christ is to demonstrate His style of dealing with anger as you encounter it at home, at the office, in your neighborhood, or wherever you are.

If you draw on His Spirit to acknowledge, process, and control your anger, you will stand out—as my friend Dan does—as a shining example of the power of Jesus Christ. And when others see that strength, coupled with gentle kindness, they'll know it has a supernatural source. They'll see you not as a warrior, not as a wimp, but rather as a peacemaker who reflects Christ's controlled, balanced style of confrontation. And they'll want to be that way, too.

Applying the Antidote

Here's a simple exercise to start you on the road to more balanced processing of your anger. Take a moment now to follow these following guidelines as you say a simple prayer:

- First, thank God for giving you emotions that help you feel with His heart—even angry feelings.
- Second, praise Him for nontoxic anger that promotes healthy, righteous change.
- Third, ask God to give you greater control when you are inappropriately angry. Invite Him to take over in those situations and use you as a living picture of His power at work in you.

For: Anger

"Everyone should be quick to listen, slow to speak, and slow to become angry, for man's anger does not bring about the righteous life that God desires."

—JAS 1:19 (NIV)

Chapter 6

Toxic Discouragement

ॐ

Sick depressed anxious
Fatigued frustrated
Puzzled perplexed lonely
Desperate despairing
Lord, for this I have you.

—Ruth Harms Calkin

ॐ

I ONCE HEARD A STORY about a mother of eight who came home one day to find her youngest five children out in the yard huddled together. As she walked over to see what was going on, she discovered they were playing with five baby skunks. Horrified, she shouted, "Run, children, run!" And so they did—each clutching a terrified baby skunk.

Can you imagine five kids, each running in a different direction—squeezing a squirming baby skunk? I'm pretty sure skunks don't like to be squeezed.

Sometimes we have problems that are like baby skunks. The more we cling to them, the more unpleasant they get. Before long, we find ourselves plummeting into a spiral of despair and discouragement. This syndrome describes what I call "toxic discouragement."

It's the kind of discouragement a single mother feels as she struggles to be both mom and dad to her children. Fatigue, stress, financial struggles—you name a problem, she has it. Sometimes she has only ten dollars in her checking account—and a week left until payday. Those are the times when unexpected needs always arise:

school fees, a trip to the doctor, a birthday party. Some days she doesn't think she'll ever see her kids grown and on their own. Even worse, some days she just doesn't care.

It's the discouragement so familiar to a couple with a rebellious teenage son. For more than a decade they've centered their lives around this boy, who means more to them than anything. They've sacrificed much to provide every possible advantage and opportunity to help him grow, thrive, and realize his hopes and dreams. They've been model Christian parents, but they feel like miserable failures. With longing, they recall the days when their little boy climbed up in their lap with a storybook, and whispered "I love you" as they tucked him into bed. Now he doesn't come home for days at a time. And when he is home, they see malice and hatred in his eyes—and in his actions.

It's the discouragement of a husband whose wife is battling terminal cancer. She's the one who's sick. She's the one who prays that God will let her live to see her children grown, but knows instinctively that she'll lose the fight before she has a chance to hold a grandchild. Still, he's the caretaker, the one who cracks jokes and puts up a good front to encourage her. He acts like he isn't scared to death even as his heart breaks a little bit more each day. He watches her fade away until he can barely see a shadow of the beautiful woman whose sparkling eyes and feisty personality once charmed the sense out of him. What happened to their plans to grow old together?

Down, Down, Down!

Maybe you have suffered a deep emotional or physical wound and you are struggling to cope with it. God wants you to be victorious over this struggle, but Satan likes to pull out the tool of discouragement and bring you down.

Discouragement is one of Satan's most often-used tools. He seems to know that if he gets us down about that one thing that's so important to us, discouragement will spread like cancer, and render us useless—to God, to others, even to ourselves.

A discouraged Christian is an ineffective Christian. You see, discouragement is one of the most deadly toxins a Christian experiences. But we are not left defenseless against it. We can discover the secrets of godly encouragement. When we do, something begins to shine within us. We experience the light of God's Spirit within us. As He fills us, that light radiates out of us in a way that is lovely and winsome to others, even in the tough times.

We can learn some of these important lessons from the Old Testament prophet Nehemiah. But before we look more closely, we need to set the scene.

In 586 B.C., Israel was conquered by Babylon, which is present-day Iraq. The Jews were taken into captivity and the walls of Jerusalem were destroyed. About a hundred and fifty years later, a man named Nehemiah led a small, determined group of Israelites back from exile. Their mission was to rebuild the walls of God's city. That's where we tune in.

In Nehemiah 4, it says that the little band was excited and zealous, energized by a high purpose—at firs. But about halfway through the rebuilding project, discouragement set in.

What was the cause of their discouragement? Mud. They got stuck in the mud and simply stopped working. And that would have been the end of the project if it weren't for Nehemiah. Here was a man who knew how to apply certain principles—the "antidotes" for discouragement. Let's take time to examine the causes of discouragement that the Israelites encountered.

Destructive Criticism

Nehemiah's report tells us that the initial cause of discouragement for the Israeli builders was criticism:

> Sanballat was very angry when he learned that we were rebuilding the wall. He flew into a rage, and insulted and mocked us, and so did his friends and the Samaritan army officers. "What does this bunch of poor, feeble Jews think they are doing," he scoffed. "Do they think they can build the wall in a day if they offer enough sacrifices?" (Neh 4:1–2, LB)

Once Sanballat started the ball rolling, others joined in the taunts. Have you ever seen what happens to a child on the playground when he drops the ball and one cruel playmate starts to taunt him? Pretty soon the whole team is hurling accusations, and the face of the child falls. He couldn't throw that ball if his life depended on it. That's about the way the Jews felt. What began as an expedition of joy became a mission of misery.

We'd all do well to take note of this: There is nothing like criticism to take the joy out of life. Criticism makes us vulnerable to discouragement.

The Halfway Syndrome

As Nehemiah's account continues, we learn the second reason why the returning Jews became discouraged: "At last the wall was completed to half its original height around the entire city—for the workers worked hard" (Neh 4:6).

Have you ever come midway through a task and just felt stumped? I call this the "halfway syndrome." Maybe it's a professional or personal project. Or maybe you stop in the middle of a personal struggle, such as overcoming an addiction or disability. Perhaps it happens while you're trying to reach a professional goal you've set for yourself.

In any case, it seems we sometimes hit a plateau when we get halfway to the finish line. And that's when discouragement sets in.

Opposition

There's probably nothing more discouraging than opposition from other people—and that's the third factor that contributed to the discouragement of the returning Jews. As they proceeded with the task of repairing the walls of Jerusalem, the local folk got pretty steamed—so much so that "they all plotted together to come and fight against Jerusalem and stir up trouble" (Neh 4:8).

But Nehemiah had the "right stuff" in the face of opposition—a balanced approach that involved prayer and action. He and his crew prayed to God and also took practical steps, posting a guard day and night to meet the threat. This is recorded in Neh 4:9—one of my favorite verses in scripture because of the balanced example it sets for us as Christians.

God wants us to be spiritually connected to Him through prayer, but He does not want us to neglect to use the physical and mental capabilities He has given us to solve our own problems. This reminds me of the old Revolutionary War saying, "Trust the Lord, but keep the powder dry." Or perhaps another saying, which goes, "Pray as if it all depends on God, but work as though it all depends on you." That's a dynamic combination—God's power channeled through human hands. Nothing can stop it—not even the opposition of enemies.

Weakened Warriors

As you can imagine, intense criticism, fatigue, and opposition eventually began to take a physical toll on the Jews. Neh 4:10 records that the strength of the laborers gave out. In the original Hebrew, this verse includes the concept of a person who has carried a heavy load for a long time, so that his legs actually begin to buckle under him. If you have ever moved from one house to another, lifting and positioning furniture and heavy boxes all day long, you may have experienced this kind of weakness. After so long, your knees actually begin to tremble. That's what happened to Nehemiah and the other laborers as they rebuilt the temple. They were trembling under their load and there was so much rubble left to face. It must have been totally overwhelming, and I'm sure the discouragement among the troops was heavy. Physical stress and fatigue will do that to you.

During the Gulf War, I heard several strategists talk about the tactic of dropping bombs during the night. They admitted that the night bombings prior to the ground offensive weren't all that helpful; it was harder to hit the targets at night, for one thing. But the reason they continued was to keep the enemy awake—to deprive them of sleep so that they were weary and stressed out. When people are in this condition, they become discouraged and unable to fight back. Sure enough, this is what happened when our troops launched the ground offensive later.

God obviously knew what He was doing when He established "the sabbath principle." We work at peak efficiency when we take one day out of seven and devote it to rest, to a change of pace, and to the worship of our Creator. When we observe this principle, we actually accomplish more during the other six days. And this helps prevent the poison of discouragement from growing within.

Once I heard InterVarsity Christian Fellowship leader Paul Little speak at a missions conference in Illinois. I was impressed by his advice to get a straight twelve hours of sleep before ever making any major life decision. When we try to make decisions without resting well, our judgment can be greatly impaired.

Too Discouraged to See Straight

When all the factors we've discussed took their toll in Nehemiah, the Jews fell into such a state of discouragement that they lost sight of their original vision. They had come to rebuild the wall. They had come with determination, energy, and enthusiasm. But now the laborers' strength was giving out and they no longer believed they could rebuild the wall.

This makes me think of many a Saturday morning that I've gone out to clean my garage, raring to go. But when I have opened the door and seen the piles of rubble and the dusty cabinets, all I have done is slam the door shut and said, Scarlett O'Hara–style, "I'll think about that later. Tomorrow's another day!"

I realize facing a messy garage is not exactly the same type of discouragement the Jews were undergoing. The point I want to make is that if we focus on the rubble—whether we're building a wall, cleaning our garage, or facing the daily struggles of life—we'll lose sight of the vision of victory that is the key to finishing the task at hand. And as we lose our vision, we also lose our confidence, which is just what happened to the Israelites.

Let's stop for a moment and take note of the downward spiral we see in this example from Nehemiah. The contributing factors that led to crippling discouragement came one by one. It was a process that fed upon itself. Criticism, fatigue, opposition, weakness, loss of vision, loss of confidence. As these factors built on one another, discouragement deepened in the work camp. And there was more to come.

The Power of Negative Thinking

The Jews were as low as they could go. That's when negative thinking threatened to blow the expedition off the charts. What a pitiful sight this was to their leader, Nehemiah, who had spearheaded the project. Thank goodness he was a man who knew how to apply biblical principles and to inspire others to follow his lead.

Let me challenge you to stop right now and think for a moment. Is there a half-built wall in your life? Can you identify that one thing that you can't seem to get on top of because you have gone down, down, down in a spiral of discouragement that has you stuck?

Is it a dream of changing careers that you've had for a long time? Perhaps you've even taken a few classes to move you in that direction, but now you've hit a plateau. Or maybe you've been asking God to start a neighborhood Bible study or even to open a door into some sort of ministry work. You've thought about it so much you know every step it would take to make it happen, but you hesitate to move forward.

What about that plan to start a family that you put on hold to go to work? When will you be ready to have that family?

Your dream—your plan—remains "half built." Hold that thought as we consider some of the strategies Nehemiah adopted to help his crew overcome discouragement and finish their job. You can apply the same strategies to your situation and get back on top of things before you know it.

Strategy #1: Two Is Better Than One

The first thing Nehemiah did to overcome discouragement in his troops was to reunite them behind their common vision or purpose. He began by positioning the people all around the wall. Then he reminded them that they need not be afraid of the enemy surrounding them. "Remember the Lord who is great and awesome," he said (Neh 4:14). They had been appointed to their task by the King of kings, and no enemy was great enough to get in His way.

After this boost, Nehemiah reorganized the work plan so that it would be more efficient. He grouped the people in family units so that they would always be functioning in a framework of support, love, and encouragement. Then he cultivated within these individual units a powerful corporate vision that fueled their determination to finish what they had started.

You know, when people unite together with a common vision for a God-appointed ministry, things are bound to happen.

Daniel Brown, a California pastor, once said that "leadership is cultivating in people today a willingness on their part to follow you into something new, for the sake of something great." That's exactly the kind of leader Nehemiah was when he challenged his people to unite and finish building the wall. He called them to follow him, for the sake of their great and mighty God.

Strategy #2: Heavenly Perspective

I can relate to the Jews as they looked around at the rubble and wondered how they could ever build a wall in the midst of such a mess. Sometimes I get bogged down in this way too. As pastor of a large church in an urban community, I am called to be a spiritual leader to several thousands of people. Many of them are struggling to cope with very difficult situations. Their lives seem to be falling down, like the Jerusalem wall. My heart breaks for them, and it would be easy for discouragement to render me useless to them.

To combat this I've come up with a little spiritual exercise you may find helpful. When I'm feeling particularly overwhelmed and discouraged, I slip outside after the sun goes down and take a few minutes to gaze up at the stars. As I do, I think of how each one of those tiny, glistening specks is actually a whole "sun" in itself, sur-rounded by a solar system. Some of those celestial bodies are far, far away—so far it's beyond my comprehension.

I once read an article about how an astronomer estimates that there are fourteen quadrillion stars in the universe. That's fourteen with fifteen zeros behind it. The prophet Isaiah writes in awe that God measured out the universe with His very own hands, and those same holy hands "weigh" the tallest, broadest mountains (Isa 40:12). Isaiah goes on to remind us that such a mighty, sovereign God can surely be trusted to care for us. These moonlight reflections really help me put my chaotic life in perspective, and then my personal problems seem more manageable.

But sometimes problems come at us early in the morning, and there are no starry skies on which to reflect. Unfortunately, the natural tendency of humans is to run away from God when facing discouraging problems. Bad move.

Any firefighter will tell you it's a deadly choice to run if your clothing catches on fire. Instead of running, you should "stop, drop, and roll." That's also what you should do when you are discouraged. Instead of running from God next time, stop, drop to your knees in prayer, and roll into His big, strong capable arms. He'll help you get a better perspective—a heavenly one—on your problems.

A construction crew was building a beautiful structure in Europe. Someone asked one of the crew members what he was doing. He replied that he was laying a brick. But when another member of the crew contemplated the very same question, he reported that he was building a cathedral. The second man had a far-reaching vision that made his work much more exciting and meaningful.

Today you may be discouraged because you feel as if you are just "laying bricks," but you're not. If you are a parent, you are not just changing diapers; you are building a young life into God's King-dom. If you are doing a job for God—any job—your work is of eter-nal importance to Him. He is the Master Architect, and we need to stay focused on the bigger picture of what He is doing through us and in us.

Strategy #3: Don't Lose Your Balance

Staying focused is a must when you are on God's construction crew. So is keeping your balance. Nehemiah knew the importance of this, so he instructed his workers to work with one hand and to hold a defensive weapon in the other.

Sometimes Christians take the approach that the world is a terrible, sinful place and, therefore, we must retreat from it. I don't think that's what God wants us to do. I think God expects us to tackle whatever He has given us to do—in the world. How else can we have an impact on others spiritually? But we must not go at our worldly work without taking with us the weapons of spiritual warfare.

Strategy #4: Have a Plan of Defense

What kind of defense shall we take with us into the world?

Nehemiah instructed his people to sound a trumpet whenever they were under attack so that others could rally in their support. Likewise, we also need to "sound the alarm" when we need spiritual support. How can anyone around us know we are feeling discouraged if we never let on that we are downhearted?

Sometimes Christians feel inhibited about calling for help from the spiritual troops. But this is a necessary first step in a plan of defense to keep us from sinking into a pit of despair. Also crucial to our spiritual strategy is the practice of studying God's Word and establishing a practice of personal, daily prayer.

Strategy #5: Serving Others Saves the Day

One more, very essential element needs to be part of the plan of defense, and Nehemiah again provides us with an example to follow.

One of the most dangerous off-shoots of discouragement is the tendency to become self-focused and absorbed, and at one point Nehemiah's troops fell into this syndrome. When they did, he challenged them to get busy helping other people, because he knew this would help them forget about their own problems. When we follow this example and encourage others, it's amazing how we are lifted above our problems and how we can let criticism roll off our backs.

Strategy #6: Let Criticism Become a Benefit

Criticism can even benefit us in a couple of ways. For example, it can be an opportunity to sharpen our spiritual perspective. When we are open to criticism—even embrace it, rather than fight it—it can help us fine-tune the "vision" God has given us. It may cause us to ask, "Is this just an idea that I have? Something that I want to do? Or is this the Lord's idea?"

When Nehemiah's crew was under critical scrutiny, I'm sure he did some pretty intensive self-evaluation. "Are we rebuilding the walls of Jerusalem just because I had the idea to do it, or because God called us to do it?" he might have asked. This process renewed Nehemiah's conviction that what the Israelites were doing was divinely appointed. Therefore, they could move ahead in spite of the destructive criticism. If we approach criticism in a similar way, we can also move ahead and grow through adversity.

Another blessing comes when we go down on our knees in response to criticism. Think, for a moment, about the person in your life who is most critical of you. My guess would be that you spend a lot of time praying about your struggles with that person. Prayer changes things, and anything that drives us into conversation with God is ultimately a good thing.

What's the Bottom Line?

What's discouraging you as you read this today? Are you burdened financially? Are you worn down and worn out by the stress of life in the fast lane? Are your children driving you crazy?

Let me encourage you to recognize that, in due time, the problems you are struggling with will pass—every last one of them. But it will be easier to get through your struggles if you stay close to God while they endure.

Have you ever seen one of those pictures that have a bigger picture hidden within a series of repetitive, colorful graphics? At first the picture appears to be a pleasant, decorative design without much more to it. But if you focus on the picture and concentrate, a more intricate "hidden" image emerges.

Life is kind of like that sometimes. Day after day of "sameness" can make you feel insignificant. But as you focus on God and concentrate on His Word, you see His carefully planned, customized picture for your life begin to emerge.

Let me encourage you with words from another godly leader. It was Joshua who said, "Be strong and of good courage; do not be afraid, nor be dismayed, for the Lord your God is with you wherever you go" (Josh 1:9).

God will go with you. He has a plan in mind for you, just as He did for Nehemiah and the crew of wall-builders. All He asks is that you keep your focus on Him and concentrate on His directions. As you do, the darkness of discouragement will give way to confident enthusiasm, and nothing will be able to stop you from finishing your wall.

Applying the Antidote

A practical antidote for discouragement is encouragement. So to get you through life's rainy days, I recommend a personal "perks file." Here's how it works:

Remember the last time someone surprised you with a special card or an unexpected phone call, just to let you know they care? How about the time your boss went out of his way to affirm you for a job well done? What about that unforgettable time when your kids brought you breakfast in bed? If we think about it, God often gives us treasured moments to let us know we are "one-of-a-kind" to Him.

Next time He sends you one of these rare moments, capture it. Record it on a card and stick it in your "perks file." Then when discouragement dumps a load on you and you're spiraling downward, revel in the treasures you've tucked away. Your file will help you stand strong and confident, even during the most discouraging times.

For: Discouragement

"... in all these things we are more than conquerors through Him who loved us."

—ROM 8:37 (NIV)

Chapter 7

Toxic Jealousy

AN ANCIENT FABLE goes something like this:

Satan and several of his demon friends are crossing the Libyan desert when they come across a very godly man. The man lives alone, fasting and praying, day after day.

You shall not covet ... anything that belongs to your neighbor.

EXOD 20:17 (NIV)

Fasting and praying are activities that always rub Satan and his pals the wrong way, so they decide to have a free-for-all with this righteous guy.

First the demons try every possible temptation of the flesh to distract the man from his meditation time. They try greed, lust, anger—everything they can think of. But nothing works.

Finally, Satan pushes them aside and takes charge. Drawing near to the man, he whispers in his ear, "Have you heard the news? Your brother was just appointed to be bishop of Alexandria."

At once, a dark, ugly look comes across the holy man's face—the look of malignant jealousy—and Satan begins to reel in his victim.

This may be a fictional story, but it targets one of Satan's favorite true-life tactics. He loves to make us jealous of one another. Jealousy is one of the most effective poisons the enemy can employ to rob us of happiness, destroy our peace of mind, make us ungrateful toward God, and damage our interpersonal relationships.

God's Take on Jealousy

We know that jealousy is one of the issues God is most concerned about. He included it in His select list of "do nots"—the Ten Commandments (Exod 20:17). God has been arbitrating jealousy since the Garden of Eden, and it can be argued that jealousy was a contributing factor to Adam and Eve's fall into sin.

When the serpent tempted Eve, he convinced her that to eat the forbidden fruit would make her "like God" (Gen 3:5). In essence, Eve coveted what God had forbidden to her. When she allowed her desire to be godlike to get the best of her, she sinned.

Jealousy is one of the most deadly spiritual toxins, and it is very important that we look to the Bible for the proper treatment. Family feuds that last for generations have been caused because brothers and sisters coveted each other's possessions, successes, looks, talents, and opportunities. Jealousy causes social and racial snobbery that can escalate into devastating hatred and violence. Throughout history, it has been a theme behind works of literature, art, and music. And hardly a day goes by that the morning news doesn't include a breaking story of an ex-spouse or lover whose jealousy spun out of control, resulting in a heinous murder or suicide.

A Closer Look at the Green-Eyed Monster

Thousands of years ago, King Solomon pinpointed the problem of jealousy when he observed that "all labor and all achievement spring from man's envy of his neighbor" (Eccl 4:4). These wise words are a concise description of "the race-horse mentality." You see, there's something deep within the psyche of a horse—a drive to stay ahead of other horses. As they run the course or the racetrack, there is a compulsion within each animal to keep his nose ahead of the horses on either side.

The same is true of human beings. When sin entered the world by man's invitation, so did a vicious universal motive. That motive is jealousy, and it drives us to try to be one step ahead of Mr. Jones, on our left, or Mrs. Smith, on our right—just like a driven racehorse.

If you are a business professional or an athlete, I can hear you saying, "I object!" A competitive nature can be a good thing, as long as it is kept in its place. But if you have ever wrestled with jealousy, you know the competitive spirit can also become a vicious tyrant, robbing us of joy, inner peace, and friendship. It can cause us to lose perspective and do malicious things that we would not otherwise do.

Have you ever worked with someone who resorted to hurtful tactics to push others off the corporate ladder in order to climb to the top? When you were a teenager, did anyone in your circle of friends ever start a vicious rumor in order to gain votes in a student election? And what about those caring parents who turn into fist-shaking maniacs when their children are bumped off the lineup at a Little League or soccer game?

The Bible teaches that jealousy is sometimes the core motive from which other motives spring. This is the underlying thought in Jeremiah's lament that "the heart is deceitful above all things and beyond cure" (Jer 17:9).

Jealousy can be very dangerous when it is so subtle within us that we don't acknowledge it, even after we become Christians. You see, when we are born again, the obvious stuff gets dealt with right away as we yield our will to the Lord. But we still have human tendencies that God must go after with a flashlight, so to speak. As we allow the Holy Spirit to shine His light into the crevices of our heart, He reveals imperceptible attitudes and motives, such as jealousy, that must be uprooted.

The Bible teaches that jealousy will destroy us if we don't deal with it. Throughout scripture, God gives us plenty of warnings that jealousy is a very serious matter to Him and that one day we will be called to account for it. He is concerned about jealousy not just because it can motivate us to harm others, but also because it harms the soul. When jealousy gets hold of us, it destroys our inner peace by causing us to obsess on our desires. Whenever we are in this kind of state, our minds are not stayed upon God, and that's when we are most vulnerable to Satan's attacks.

Killing the "Monster"

To put an end to the "green-eyed monster" of jealousy, we must first determine where it comes from. Jealousy grows from four wrong mental perceptions that are deeply imprinted on our hearts.

The first is a deflated self-image. We are jealous of others because we don't realize and appreciate our own value. We forget so easily that God, the sovereign Creator, made each of us unique.

Stop and think for a moment. Do you realize that there is no other person in history exactly like you? You have a combination of qualities that makes you one of a kind, and nobody can fill your designated spot in the universe. When you acknowledge this—really grasp it—then the need to compete with others vanishes.

The second mental perception that feeds jealousy is an inflated ego. Paul bluntly warns us not to think more highly of ourselves than we ought to (Rom 12:3). Peter learned from his own painful struggle with an inflated ego how God requires that we humble ourselves before Him (1 Pet 5:6).

Sometimes, in order to cover up our feelings of inadequacy, we overinflate our areas of adequacy. Simply put, we become arrogant fools. We look for someone who can't compete with us in a particular area and we compare ourselves to that person because it makes us look good. It's a dangerous game, because bragging and calling attention to ourselves in this way offends people. An inflated ego leads to jealous competition that will eventually isolate us from others and put a damper on our relationship with God. Instead, we need to acknowledge that God knows what He's doing and He designed us the way we are because it is the best possible way for us to be.

A third root cause of jealousy is a twisted perception of God's justice. Perhaps we're angry with Him because we feel He has dealt unfairly with us—not given us what we "deserve," or allowed hard things to happen to us that we feel we don't deserve. As we compare our circumstances with those of other people, we may even accuse God of playing favorites or picking on us.

I've noticed that we tend to have the same sort of attitude toward God as we do about umpires. When an umpire makes a call against a favorite team, we tend to cry, "Unfair!" There is an inherent suspicion that authority figures rule against us more than for us, and we expect God to act in a similar way. We've bought into Satan's accusation that God loves other people more than He loves us, and if we don't check that attitude early, it will kill our sense of gratitude toward our Maker. We can't be thankful for what God has done for us if we are obsessed with what He has not done for us.

A fourth root cause of toxic jealousy is spiritual insecurity. We analyze God's feelings for us by external rather than internal evidences of His love. Have you ever noticed, though, that God often allows the external blessings to be taken away from a believer in order to develop an inner spiritual grace and security that can never be taken away?

A perfect example is the life of Joni Eareckson Tada. When Joni was a teenager, she became paralyzed in a diving accident. She was young and beautiful, healthy and vital. Yet in one brief moment her hopes, dreams, and plans seemed to be blotted out forever. Now, years later, Joni inspires and challenges people around the world through her amazing gift for drawing beautiful pictures using a brush held between her teeth. Her wisdom, gained through her trust of God in the midst of loss, is recorded in books bearing her name that help others to overcome adversity. She is happily married, a sought-out speaker—a woman with a full life and a fruitful ministry.

The Bible gives us many examples of people God allowed hardship to come upon in order to shine more brightly through them. Think of the trials of Job, the injustices committed against Joseph, the sufferings of Paul. These men gained precious spiritual strength and intimacy with God, not because He gave them things, but because He allowed things to be taken away from them to show that He was all-sufficient for their needs.

When our perception of who we are is anchored in the love and affirmation of Jesus Christ, it frees us from the tyranny of toxic jealousy. And then we are free to enjoy even more the tangible blessings God chooses to bestow on us. This is because we no longer measure ourselves by what we have, but rather by who we are in Christ. Keeping up with Mr. Jones or Mrs. Smith is no longer so important.

Thirty-one Flavors . . . and Counting

If you are like me, then you enjoy an occasional trip to Baskin-Robbins for a scoop or two of their long list of ice cream choices. Just about as many varieties of jealousy exist, but they don't taste like gourmet ice cream. Let's take a look at six varieties of jealousy that can poison our lives.

Variety #1: Jealousy of Someone's Honor

This is the first manifestation of jealousy we see in biblical history. It comes up four chapters into Genesis. God asked Cain and Abel to bring Him an offering, and He told them exactly what to bring.

Abel obeyed, but Cain brought a substitute offering of his own choosing. He thought his sacrifice was better than the one God had asked for, but what God really wanted from Cain and Abel was obedience. When God affirmed and honored Abel for doing well, Cain could not stand it. Jealousy became hatred and finally turned into deadly rage—resulting in the first act of murder.

Variety #2: Jealousy of a Family Member

We see an example of family jealousy in a tale of two sisters, Leah and Rachel. You can find the story in Genesis 30, where we learn that Leah and Rachel were both married to the same man. Can you imagine sibling rivalry combined with romantic competition? This scene is a setup for disaster.

Actually, the story of Leah and Rachel is a good illustration of several related strains of jealousy. It typifies the rivalry between two siblings that can cause dissension and disharmony within a family, and also gives some particular insights into female and male envy.

In the story of Cain and Abel we saw that a desire for the highest position of honor fueled the flames of Cain's covetousness. With Leah and Rachel, it was a competition over love and family security.

Men and women have different emotional and psychological needs that have an impact on the areas where they are most vulnerable to toxic jealousy. Generally speaking, men often want to be the strongest and most powerful, whereas women want to be the most beautiful and capable. A woman may desire to be "Mother of the Year," while a man (and sometimes a woman) might covet a professional title such as "president" or "chairman of the board."

Variety #3: Jealousy of Righteousness

Are you surprised by this one? Even though immorality seems rampant today, it is nevertheless true that each of us has a yearning to please God. In fact, the teasing and jeering that Christians often endure at the hands of unbelievers testifies to this yearning. People taunt us not so much because they detest us but because they are convicted by God's righteous reflection in us.

A good illustration of this is the story of Joseph, whose brothers were jealous of him for a number of reasons. The major problem was that Joseph, though very young, was obviously very close to God. His brothers resented Joseph because he was a constant reminder to them that they needed to work on their own relationship with the Lord.

Variety #4: Jealousy of Someone Who Is "Under" You

Perhaps you are thinking that this one doesn't make sense. After all, if you are in an elevated position, why would you be envious of someone "under" you?

Think again. Suppose, for example, that you are middle-aged and you've worked very hard to achieve a position of responsibility at work. Suddenly you find there's a new employee in the lunchroom when you go to get your morning cup of coffee. It seems like you are hearing this person's name every fifteen minutes—in the hallway, on the elevator, at meetings. She's a young, up-and-coming, aggressive, talented new face. And you're afraid she will push you right out of your office and into the line at the unemployment office.

This is exactly how Saul felt. He was king of Israel—the most powerful man alive. Along came David, a mere kid. Saul felt threatened, and a vicious, destructive jealousy took hold that eventually destroyed him—and caused much hurt and unhappiness to others, as well.

One of the saddest things about Saul's jealousy is that it was needless. David was not seeking to usurp Saul in any way. In fact, David was devoted to Saul. If Saul had recognized and affirmed this, David's support would have enhanced and strengthened his reign. Instead, Saul allowed paranoia to grow into destructive jealousy, and we need to be forewarned by his example.

Variety #5: Jealousy of Someone Who Is "Over" You

This type can be equally as destructive as its counterpart. In Psalm 106 we sense the envy of Miriam and Aaron toward their brother Moses. Even though he was younger, Moses was called by God to an important position of leadership that placed his siblings in subservience to him.

Often when someone close to us is in an elevated position, we tend to be envious of the "perks" that go with it. We forget the drawbacks and sacrifices that are called for. If you study the life of Moses, you will see that leadership was very difficult for him—at times, a real burden. Yet his brother and sister were extremely jealous.

A tragic example of this type of jealousy took place once in our community. A woman employed by a local department store graciously befriended a younger male employee, encouraging him and giving him rides to work when needed. She was trying to help the young man as much as she could, but when she received a promotion instead of him, the young man became enraged. He came to the worksite with a gun and shot her and another employee, killing them both. He was only nineteen, but in a single moment of jealous rage, he essentially ended three lives, including his own.

Variety #6: Jealousy of Someone Used by God

Our Lord Jesus was Himself a victim of this final manifestation of jealousy. The scribes and pharisees could not receive Jesus because they were so envious of the miracles He performed and because God used Him in such a powerful way. How tragic for them. They could have chosen to support Jesus and thereby be used as partners to enhance His ministry, but instead they let envy steal the most valuable opportunity God ever gave them to serve Him.

The Cure for What Ails Us

How many times have you turned on the television just in time to hear an ad about how "early detection" of cancer is the key to beating it? The same holds true for toxic jealousy. The key to beating it is to confront it early on and then to respond by following a few practical guidelines.

Here are the powerful biblical principles that will help us deal with jealousy.

A Dose of Humility

First, apply a dose of humility every time you open your mouth. Think back to our example of Joseph, who was sold into slavery by his jealous brothers. Joseph could have avoided this unpleasant fate if only he had kept to himself his dream that he would one day rule over his brothers.

Or, to cast this into a scene more relevant to our day and time, let's just say if you have a dream that you are going to get your boss's job, it's not advisable to share that dream with your boss over lunch. I'm not advising you to be aloof or distant or to clothe yourself with false humility. I'm simply saying that it is unwise to flaunt your talents. After all, true talent will inevitably come out; it's not necessary to promote it.

Practice Affirming Others

Second, practice affirming others. This is a good preventative habit that will safeguard you from jealousy, both external and internal. Why? Because if you affirm other people's attributes and accomplishments, they will feel secure with you and will be less likely to be envious. And when you freely offer affirmation, other people will more likely affirm and applaud you, as well. The need to compete is diffused if people in relationships recognize individual talents and affirm them in one another.

No Fear

A third preventative practice is to deal with fear and paranoia early on. When you see signs that the green-eyed monster is threatening to cause problems between you and another person, doesn't it make sense to put a little distance between the two of you? If someone is exhibiting jealousy toward you, or if you feel it rising within yourself toward another person, get apart for a while. A little time and space can change our perspective and empower us to deal with toxic feelings of envy.

Turn the Other Cheek

Finally, scripture teaches you to "bless those who persecute you" and to "overcome evil with good" (Rom 12:14, 21).

You might say. "I'm only human, you know." True, but as a born-again child of God you have His divine Spirit living inside of you. You can draw on Him to rise above your "only human" tendencies and to help you respond in a supernatural way. It won't be an easy pill to swallow at times, but it is possible to submit our human emotions to our super-human Lord. And if you make a choice to apply this biblical antidote, I promise you there is life—blessed life, indeed—after jealousy.

Applying the Antidote

The best way I know to keep yourself from coveting what you don't have is to focus on what you do have. Next time you struggle with envy, make a "Blessings List."

1. Take a piece of paper and a pencil and go into your kitchen. Look around and make a list of everything you see that you have to be thankful for.

2. Every time you write something down, say an arrow prayer of praise. For example, "Thank you, God, that I have clean, running water in my home, to drink, to bathe in, for cooking." Then say, "I praise you, Lord, that you have given me a job so I can provide for my family." And on and on.

3. Move from room to room with your "Blessing List." God inhabits praise, and as you thank Him for what He has given you, He will help you relinquish the toxic jealousy that is so destructive to you and to other people.

For: Jealousy

" . . . be content with what you have . . . "

—HEB 13:5 (NIV)

Chapter 8

Toxic Worry

ॐ

*Worry is like a rocking chair:
it gives you something to do
but doesn't get you anywhere.*

—Anonymous

ॐ

The manager of a hotel in Raleigh, North Carolina, remembers the night he heard screams coming from one of the rooms. "It's in the phone book! It's in the phone book!" The cry came again and again, awakening the other guests and causing a loud commotion.

Alarmed and curious, the manager called the house detective, and they cautiously entered the room together. They found the screams were coming from a man who was fast asleep. They woke him and asked, "Why are you screaming?" The embarrassed hotel guest explained, "I dreamed that the IRS wanted to send me a big refund, but they had lost my address."

The IRS, your health, your future, your kids, what haunts your dreams? Are you a person who frets and worries from the minute you wake up until you drift off to sleep at night?

We may be amused by the hotel dreamer, but our dreams can be good indicators of what we have on our minds. Although we need to be careful not to overanalyze them and certainly not rely on them for guidance without God's confirmation, examining our dreams can reveal some helpful insights into our subconscious fears.

95

For example, I recall that before our daughter Abigail was born, my wife, Kimberly, had a dream that she gave birth to a litter of kittens. (Now there's an unrealistic fear!) And for fifty years after his graduation from college, my dad had a recurring dream that he was walking exuberantly into his very last class only to find, to his horror, that he was supposed to have been attending lab sessions for that class all semester.

The dream that haunts me most is one in which I'm standing before my congregation on Sunday morning, ready to preach, when suddenly I glance down to see that I'm dressed in my pajamas. These dreams are so absurd they make us laugh, but it's pretty obvious that they reveal our insecurities. Psychologists call them "anxiety dreams."

Like a compass needle that always points north, does your mind constantly return to that one thing that robs you of inner peace and security, even when you are sleeping? Be comforted. You are not alone.

Test Yourself

Here's a little test. Read through the list below and put a checkmark by the categories that you might worry about. Then rate yourself on a scale of one to ten—one being "no worries" and ten being "worrier of the year." Here goes:

__ Finances	__ Children
__ Salvation	__ Tax returns
__ Health	__ Relationships
__ Failure	__ Household maintenance
__ Reputation	__ Natural disasters
__ End of the world	__ Making wrong decisions

Whether you marked one or all the categories on the list, I'm certain there are areas of worry in your life. The purpose of this test is to make you aware of a process that is so normal and commonplace that you may not recognize it as a potential problem in your life.

Whether it is suppressed, as in our dreams, or in the forefront of our thoughts during every waking moment, worry is a basic human tendency. If it spins out of control, worry can be one of the deadliest of spiritual toxins, so let's learn how to rein it in.

God's Word on Worry

What does the Bible say about worry? First, it says that worry, in excess, can be a sin. Jesus talked about this on several occasions. Whenever He did, it was with an attitude of gentle compassion that demonstrated His understanding of worry as a condition that is common to men and women. His counsel was firm, but always hopeful and intent on encouraging and developing faith and trust.

On one occasion, Jesus was visiting with Mary and Martha, sisters who were His special friends. "Martha, Martha, you are worried and bothered about so many things; but only few things are necessary, really only one" (Luke 10:41). Jesus' words to Martha that day were a gentle rebuke because she was so preoccupied with preparations and appearances that she couldn't relax long enough to sit down and enjoy the one really important thing—her precious time with Him.

Another time Jesus spoke about worry was in the Sermon on the Mount. This time He confronted the human tendency to worry over possessions. In a nonjudgmental way, Jesus pointed out to those around Him that even the birds and the flowers are clothed beautifully by God's hand. He said, "But if God so arrays the grass in the field . . . how much more will He clothe you, O men of little faith! And do not seek what you shall eat, and what you shall drink, and do not keep worrying" (Luke 12:28–29, NASB). Essentially Jesus was saying that to continue worrying when God shows you He will provide is a lack of trust—a weakness of faith. It is significant that He ended the discussion with a command: "Do not keep worrying!"

Calling It as God Sees It

If you are like me, you think of sins in categories. There are the lesser "nickel and dime sins," and the more serious, costly ones. Most of us probably think of worry as a minor sin. It's not like cheating, stealing, or killing, and in a sense it even seems to be a form of "nurturing."

But for some of us worry is an obsession. Maybe we are addicted to worry about only one certain thing. In this case, anxiety is truly a serious sin—even a deadly one. It indicates a lack of trust in God and His promises. Left unchecked, worry can harm us physically and emotionally. It can lead to stress-related diseases that prevent us from living effectively and even have the potential to kill us.

It grieves God to see His children wasting a moment of time in worry, so we need to find ways to combat this sin.

When I'm beset by worry, it helps me to imagine myself consulting with God, face-to-face. Would I dare look the Creator of the Universe in the eye and say, "I don't trust you with this worry, Lord. I'm not sure you can handle it." No, of course not. What an insult it is to Him when we lack trust in His ability to handle our worries.

Worry Will Boggle Your Mind

A second biblical insight we have into worry is that it causes us to make bad decisions. The best example of this is recorded in Genesis 12, where Abraham, patriarch of God's people, made a very poor decision that had tragic consequences because he let worry boggle his mind. In Abraham's case, as with all of us, he tried to jump out of the way of something that he really didn't need to be afraid of. Ironically, he jumped directly into the path of something he did need to be afraid of.

Abraham moved his family into the land of Egypt ruled by Pharaoh, who had a harem full of beautiful women. Fear gripped Abraham's heart because Sarah, his wife, was beautiful. He just knew that Pharaoh would want to add her to his harem. You might think that his concern would be for his wife, but Abraham was more worried for his own sake. What would happen to him? Would Pharaoh order him killed in order to have Sarah?

His anxiety over this remote possibility became so unbalanced that he ultimately involved Sarah in a serious lie. "Say that you are my sister, so that I will be treated well," he said to the woman he was supposed to love, honor, and lead in righteousness. What a terrible thing to do. And viewed within the context of the whole story of Abraham's life, it gets even worse. Just prior to this, God had called Abraham and told him that He had special plans for him and the descendants who would come through him. He was a man who walked and talked with God, but worry caused him to forget the sovereign power of his divine Friend and to make a foolish decision. It was one that nearly had disastrous results. Sure enough, Pharaoh took poor Sarah into his harem.

At first, it seemed to Abraham that he had made a good decision, since he was treated well for Sarah's sake. In fact, Abraham acquired sheep and cattle, camels, and servants, all because Pharaoh thought he was Sarah's brother. But God's anger burned over this unrighteous situation, and He inflicted Pharaoh's household with a serious plague. Somehow Pharaoh, who was not a believer, figured out what was going on. He immediately summoned Abraham and said, "What have you done to me? Why did you tell me she was your sister so that I took her to be my wife?"

Now we reach the part of this intriguing tale that always astounds me. Instead of ordering Abraham to be killed, or even stripped of his wealth and banished, Pharaoh returned Sarah to him and instructed him to take all of his possessions and go. He even provided body-guards to usher them on their way.

What a guy, you say? Yes, but not Pharaoh. It was God who showed the vastness of His mercy and grace toward Abraham and his family by moving Pharaoh to release them. It was God who proved His faithfulness as a promise-keeper who would see them through this and give them the land and the family He had pledged to them, even though they did not deserve it. And the good news for us is that Abraham's God is the same Lord who promises to see us through. This story is a good one to remember when we are tempted to take matters into our own hands and try to sidestep something we are worried about.

Worry Will Come Back to Haunt You

If the story ended here, it might be like one of those fairy tales where the hero and heroine go off and live happily ever after. But sadly, we see that Abraham repeated the same sin again later in his life (Genesis 20)—a different land, a different king, the same fear, the same deceptive lie. And once again, the same faithful God kept His promise and bailed Abraham out of a tight spot.

Perhaps you are wrestling with some issues right about now. You may be saying, "What about consequences? Doesn't sin have consequences, even for believers?" Certainly, and I'm sure there were many for Abraham that are not recorded in the biblical account, but the most tragic of all is that "toxic worry" rubbed off on his son Isaac. If we read Genesis 26 we find the same old script being performed again—only this time the protagonist is Isaac, who asks his beautiful wife, Rebekah, to be his partner in the very same deception. In this case, the old saying "like father, like son" couldn't be more applicable.

Let me summarize a few important lessons we can learn from this true story about Abraham. First of all, worry can cause us to make bad decisions that will have far-reaching consequences. Second, worry displays a lack of trust in God and tarnishes our testimony. And third, worry rubs off on other people—especially those closest to us. Like a snowball rolling downhill, worry piles sin upon sin and drags others with us in a downward slide. Do you still think that worry is a "nickel and dime" sin?

Not to Worry: Five Reasons Why

Let's turn to the New Testament and see what Jesus has to say about worry. In Matthew 6 He speaks about five ways that worry is bad for us.

Worry Prevents Us from Appreciating What We Have

Jesus says, "Therefore I tell you, do not worry about your life, what you will eat or drink; or about your body, what you will wear. Is not life more important than food, and the body more important than clothes?" (Matt 6:25). When we allow ourselves to fret over things we don't have or even to be anxious about losing the things we do have, we overlook the wealth of blessings God has given us to enjoy now. I may not have a mansion or a yacht, but I have a home for my family and there's never been a day that we haven't had food to eat. Most importantly, I have the freedom to worship and fellowship with my Savior—the richest blessing of all. When I choose to remember God's blessings, worry seems absurd.

Worry Makes Us Forget Our Value

Jesus points out that when we worry, we overlook how very important we are to God. "Look at the birds of the air," He says. "They do not sow or reap or store away in barns, and yet your Heavenly father feeds them. Are not you much more valuable than they?" (Matt 6:26)

Wow! God, who created the entire universe, knows me by name. He knows how many hairs I have on my head and the agenda for every single day of my life. In short, He considers me to be so valuable that He personally notes my every need. If I keep my relationship with Him intact, I don't feel so prone to worry because I know He cares about every detail of my life. And the same goes for you.

Worry Is Not Constructive

What can it accomplish, after all? As Jesus says, "Who of you by worrying can add a single hour to his life?" (Matt 6:27) What He is saying is that worry is a colossal waste of precious time. Not only is it not constructive, but carried to an extreme it can also become destructive.

We have the option to hand our worries over to Jesus and allow Him to show us how to take action and deal with any situation that is causing our anxiety. "Don't worry about anything, instead pray about everything." In contemporary language, this is what Paul teaches in Phil 4:6. If you are a worrier, I suggest you commit this verse to memory and attach a mental "red flag" to it. When you catch yourself fretting over something, play it through your mind over and over, and you will soon find that the Holy Spirit will come alongside and take the burden off your shoulders.

Worry Causes Us to Forget the Promises of God

I heard a story once about a time when Billy Graham was in the U.S. Senate dining room. Across the room, several senators were engaged in a lively discussion.

Finally one of them came to him and said, "Some of us are having a debate over here. As we look at the world scene, some of us are optimists and some of us are pessimists. Which are you?"

When Reverend Graham assured the senator that he was an optimist, the senator was taken aback. "How, when you look at the world today, can you be an optimist?" he challenged.

I love the answer Billy Graham gave him. He said, "I am an optimist because I have read the final page of the Bible, and God is going to win in the end." You see, when we become trapped in a state of worry, we lose track of the last page of the Bible—and all the pages that go before it that are packed with His comforting promises and a historical record of His faithfulness throughout the ages.

Worry Does Not Reflect Christ to Others

Perhaps this is the most tragic consequence of worry. Going back to Matthew, we heed again the words of Jesus: "So do not worry, saying 'What shall we eat?' or 'What shall we drink?' or 'What shall we wear?' For the pagans run after all of these things, and your heavenly Father knows that you need them" (Matt 6:31–32)

One of the most powerful testimonies you can make for Jesus Christ is not to present yourself as a problem-free person. If you really want to make a positive case for believing in Jesus, let your problems be visible to others and let them see you trusting in Him to solve them. Be different from "the pagans." People today are searching for those who have authentic faith in an authentic God. As you go through times of difficulty walking one step at a time with the Lord, you are a "visual aid" He uses to impress other people. As people observe Him working in you and through you, a real person with real problems, they will be irresistibly drawn to Him.

John Wesley, who lived in the eighteenth century and was one of the greatest evangelists of all time, was once aboard a ship destined for missionary service to Native Americans in Georgia. He was a religious man at the time, but not yet born again.

A violent storm arose and everyone on the boat thought they were doomed. Wesley was petrified, but then he noticed a small group of people, some very godly Moravians who were also on the boat. As the tempest tossed the vessel to and fro, they huddled together singing hymns. Wesley was so impressed by their calm trust that he became hungry for a faith like theirs. The inner strength and calm of these believers in the midst of a very frightening situation was something he wanted for himself, and so he began to search for the real Jesus.

Of course, John Wesley found his Savior and spent the rest of his life drawing others to Him. Dealing with worry by trusting God will attract people to Jesus like steel to a magnet.

Wise Words for the Worry-Prone

If you are a worrier, you're probably feeling a little depressed right about now. But I have good news for you: Worry is not an incurable disease. Jesus has given us two biblical antidotes with great healing power, if we choose to apply them.

Trust Builder #1: Seek God, Not Self

Jesus gives words of wisdom for the terminal worrier: "But seek first his kingdom and his righteousness, and all these things will be given to you as well" (Matt 6:33).

Perhaps you read them and say, "Aw, Jesus, couldn't You be a little more concrete? Couldn't You be a bit more practical?" But I've found that this is perhaps the most practical verse in the Bible for dealing with worry. Why?

It helps me to think of it this way: If I seek first my kingdom, doing my will my way, then worry is absolutely appropriate, because the outcome of my search is totally my responsibility. But when I seek first His way, His kingdom, His plan, His righteousness, then I can sleep like a baby at night, because the responsibility for the outcome now belongs to God. The best antidote for worry is trusting obedience.

Rom 8:28 is one of the most quoted verses of scripture, but I find that people rarely get past the first part of the verse: "And we know that in all things God works for the good . . ." But not everything does work out for good, according to our human understanding. So we need to read on to the part that says, ". . . for the good of those who love Him, who have been called according to His purpose" (Rom 8:28, NIV). Things can work out for our ultimate good only when we are obediently in the center of God's will. When we are in that special spot, we no longer need to make ourselves sick with worry. The outcome belongs to God, Who created everything and holds us in the palm of His hand.

Trust Builder #2: Just for Today

The second antidote Jesus offers us comes in the form of a command: "Therefore do not worry about tomorrow, for tomorrow will worry about itself. Each day has enough trouble of its own" (Matt 6: 34, NIV).

Sir William Osler (1849–1919), who founded the famous Johns Hopkins Medical School in Baltimore, Maryland, used a description of an ocean liner as an analogy for worry.[1] According to his description, the hull of an ocean liner has many different compartments. The vessel is carefully designed so that if it hits an iceberg or somehow gets a tear in its side and water comes rushing in, the captain can turn a series of valves to isolate the water into a particular compartment at the site of the tear. If only that compartment fills with water, the ship will not sink. But if the water spills into several of the compartments and fills the hull, the ship will go down.

Jesus' "worry principle" is sort of like the ocean liner. He tells us that God gives enough grace for one day at a time. We need to live our lives in "day-tight compartments" so the cares and worries of life do not cause us to sink into desperation. As God gave the Israelites fresh manna each morning in their wilderness journey, so He gives us grace to deal with our concerns, one day at a time.

What are you worried about today? Do you think you can handle that issue—whatever it is—until, say, midnight tonight? I bet you can. That bill that needs to be paid? Do you think you can cover it until midnight? Probably. And what about that health issue you're struggling with? Can you make it until midnight? Today's troubles are manageable. It's only when we begin to take on tomorrow's troubles, and those of a week or month from now, that we become overburdened. That's the good reason why Jesus commanded us to "not worry about tomorrow."

Worrier or Warrior?

I'll never forget Alma, a woman of faith I met when Kimberly and I flew from Miami to Colombia to adopt our two sons. We were very anxious on that flight about the task we had ahead of us. Alma spoke only Spanish, and I could not understand her very well. I remember how very nervous she was when the plane took off. To deal with her fear, Alma reached into her purse and pulled out a Spanish version of a Gideon New Testament. I watched her open to Psalm 91 as the plane took off for Colombia. It begins like this: "He who dwells in the shelter of the Most High will rest in the shadow of the Almighty. I will say of the Lord, 'He is my refuge and my fortress, my God in whom I trust'" (Ps 91:1–2, NIV).

Let me assure you, God is absolutely trustworthy. He promises to shield you from the cares of your world, but you've got to climb into His fortress. You have a standing invitation—an open door. When all is said and done, it's up to you whether you live your life as a "worrier" or a "warrior," clothed in His impenetrable armor.

Applying the Antidote

In Ps 22:3, we are told that God "inhabits" the praises of His people. Where praise is, God is. And where God is, worry isn't. A good practical weapon to use against the enemy's attack through worry is to "practice praise." You can be creative in the way you do this. Perhaps you love to sing. Sing praises to God in the shower, on the freeway, as you do your work—the possibilities are endless. Or maybe you enjoy listening to music. If so, then build a library of praise and worship CDs or tapes that you can play to lift you into the presence of God when worry is like a prisoner's ball and chain that drags you down. If you establish a habit of praise and worship, after a while it will become a way of life for you and you will find that worry becomes more manageable.

For: Worry

"Cast all your anxiety on Him because He cares for you."

—1 Pet 5:7 (NIV)

Chapter 9

Toxic Resentment

෯

See to it that no one misses
the grace of God and that
no bitter root grows up
to cause trouble . . .

—HEB 12:15 (NIV)

෯

DOUG WAS ALWAYS a very active person. He was hard-working, involved in several sports, and had a close-knit family. In fact, he had a pretty great life. But then, at age thirty, Doug was diagnosed with cancer.

The doctor ordered radiation therapy, which was successful in ridding him of the cancer. But because the radiology technician made a tragic mistake, Doug was left permanently paralyzed from the neck down.

If anyone had a legitimate reason to be bitter and resentful, it was my friend Doug. And yet, I've never met a more positive person.

To this day, whenever I spend time with him, I come away feeling encouraged. In fact, I would say Doug has a "ministry of encouragement" because he chooses to be grateful that he was cured of life-threatening cancer, rather than to be resentful that a human mistake left him disabled. He chose to forgive the technician because people make mistakes—sometimes very serious ones with long-term consequences.

Most of the time, the injuries we suffer are not caused by cruel intentions. They happen because we are human, and therefore prone to error. Or they just happen for no apparent reason at all.

Who Said Life Was Fair?

Have you ever been in an upsetting situation that is really nobody's fault? You can't lash out at your spouse or your child, or even your next-door neighbor. So you carry around a feeling of bitterness that lodges inside you and keeps you stirred up. Resentment can be a sinister poison that eats away at your soul and squelches your happiness. It can put a damper on the rest of your life unless you deal with it.

Resentment usually has very little to do with a particular situation or person. It has everything to do with attitude and perspective. Do you know someone who has experienced terrible things in life and yet, like my friend Doug, they have a positive perspective? Or on the flip side, do you know someone who is consumed with resentment even though he seems to have every advantage?

Sometimes we are like children who cry out in pain to anyone who will listen. But if someone steps in and tries to remove the source of pain, we resist and refuse the help. I personally relate to this because sometimes I catch myself complaining and whining about a hurt in my life, but when God provides someone to help me deal with it, I resist Him. I choose to hold on to my hurt, rather than release it to the One who can heal it.

Bitter or Better?

When life deals us a harsh blow, it's not the event that is of utmost importance. It is how we respond that matters. In tough times, we have a choice. We can choose to adopt either a "horizontal" or a "vertical" perspective. In simple terms, this means that we can choose to see things from a human, earthly point of view (horizontal), or from God's point of view as we look up toward Him for enlightenment (vertical).

We can choose to spend our time and energy—perhaps a whole lifetime of it—trying to find a human reason for our hurt and becoming more and more bitter and resentful over the unfairness of our situation. This is the horizontal approach. How much better it is to choose instead to release our pain to the Holy Spirit—to cast our eyes vertically toward Heaven and allow God to carry us forward in victory. Looking to the Lord for help can make the difference between our being bitter people or better people.

Nip It in the Bud

Since our response to life's knocks is the key to moving beyond them, I recommend practicing a little preventative medicine. If you know that you tend to have a horizontal perspective, then you can practice choosing the vertical response instead, to prevent being caught off-guard. So let's take a look and see how a horizontal response differs from a vertical response.

In both cases, there are several phases we pass through. A horizontal response begins with surprise and moves quickly into feelings of being hurt or attacked. Then paranoia sets in—anxious anticipation that more hurt is yet to come. Finally, fear and hurt turn to bitter resentment, and often a determination to take revenge.

A vertical response begins with trust in God, who is sovereign. No matter what happens to us, He can use it for our good. The more intimate we are in our relationship with Him, the quicker we are able to release the situation into His trustworthy hands. We acknowledge that He is in control of everything that happens and that He has promised He can and will bring good out of bad (Rom 8:28). Notice that the verse does not say that all things are good. It says that God is able to work good through them, if we place ourselves in His will and trust Him.

When we do, He gives our pain a purpose that can make all the difference in the world in how it feels to us. We can move to the next phase of expectancy—watching and waiting to see what God is teaching or showing us through the hardship we're experiencing. Finally, God will lead us to the phase of forgiveness and acceptance that allows us to grow through the hardship and move on as stronger, more mature people.

With God, Pain Has a Purpose

Keith Korstjens is my colleague and friend. He and his wife, Mary, are intimately acquainted with God's process of bringing purpose out of pain.

One Saturday morning, just four years into their marriage, Keith rushed Mary to the hospital. She was twenty-four years old, an active, healthy woman. But she had not been feeling well for a few days, and now she had a dangerously high fever. Something was not right. Keith and Mary intuitively knew this was not just a bad case of the flu. That day they learned Mary had polio—she would spend the rest of her life as a quadriplegic.

More than forty years have passed since that day, and not one of them has been wasted. There's not enough time and space here for me to tell you the details of Keith and Mary's journey together as they built a marriage and a life in a world of respirators, wheelchairs, and braces. Believe me, it is an incredible story.

Living with a handicap is never easy. The Korstjenses talk frankly about the low times—the soul-searching, the agonizing frustration, the moments when small indignities seemed too much to bear. But as Keith and Mary held tightly to each other and looked upward to God for their source of strength, they found His way of escape—moment by moment. Today they sincerely thank God for the way He has used them, individually and as a couple, to inspire, encourage, and challenge others to look for purpose in their pain. In Keith's book, *Not a Sometimes Love,* he writes:

> *[Mary is] a remarkable woman who hasn't just risen above a handicap—she has capitalized on it! She's remarkable partly because she doesn't think of herself as at all unusual. When she talks about herself, it's always in terms of being a most ordinary lady. Yet she has given me—her husband—some of life's greatest gifts as she has lived out a winner's lifestyle . . . from a wheelchair!*[1]

I realize that most of us will never be called on to endure what Keith and Mary Korstjens have experienced. But whatever we are called to endure, we can follow their inspiring example and choose to live a "winner's lifestyle" by trusting God to bring good out of our pain.

Once, Twice, Three Times a Victim

Another person who lived a winner's lifestyle was Joseph. On three separate occasions, Joseph was the victim of terrible injustice.

The first was when his older brothers conspired to sell him into slavery because of an extreme sort of sibling rivalry (Genesis 37). He became a slave in the Egyptian household of a powerful man named Potiphar. There, Joseph earned the approval of his master through his good attitude and intelligence.

Then came the second unjust blow. Joseph's youth and good looks attracted the eye of Potiphar's wife, who tried to seduce him (Genesis 39). When Joseph refused her advances out of respect for God's moral laws, she viciously turned on him and accused him of attempted rape—an accusation that landed Joseph in jail. There, he met two inmates—the chief cupbearer and the chief baker to none other than Pharaoh himself.

As you may recall, Joseph correctly interpreted a dream that the chief cupbearer would be set free. And even though the encouraged inmate gratefully promised to remember and to help Joseph once he was out of prison, he forgot his vow once he was released. Blow three for Joseph.

For two more years, he waited in prison—truly a victim of unfair abuse. But he never turned bitter or resentful. Even in a dark, depressing cell, Joseph lived a winner's lifestyle. He looked upward to God for strength and purpose and trusted Him to bring good out of bad.

Eventually the cupbearer remembered Joseph—two long years later, when Pharaoh needed someone to interpret a puzzling dream. Joseph was summoned, and Pharaoh was so impressed that he made Joseph his right hand man.

The Plot Thickens

Meanwhile, Joseph's brothers were experiencing some tough times of their own. A widespread famine threatened their lives until, in desperation, they came to Egypt to beg for help.

Guess who was in charge of doling out help? The little brother they sold into slavery years before—Joseph, who was now the second most powerful man in the world. Although his brothers did not recognize him, Joseph knew them at once. How the tables turn.

What would you have done if you had been Joseph in this interesting situation? He had been wronged not once or twice, but three times in his life. He was a prime candidate for bitterness, resentment, and justifiable revenge. Instead, Joseph's heart was broken by the sight of his struggling family.

Imagine their terror as he revealed his identity. They expected him to return evil for evil, but they were in for an amazing surprise. Because Joseph had always responded vertically, he had long ago forgiven them and had moved beyond the need for revenge. Joseph reassured them that even though they had meant to harm him, God had used it all for good.

Do you see how Joseph allowed God to use his undeserved pain for a higher purpose by sending Joseph ahead to Egypt and moving him into a position of power that eventually saved his family from starving to death? Even more importantly, Joseph's submission to God preserved the sacred human line that was God's vehicle for bringing the Messiah into the world.

A Story with a Sequel

It seems as if this should be the end of the story. Joseph saves his family. Everyone is reconciled, and they live happily ever after—right? Well, not exactly. The issue of resentment returned.

Later, when Joseph's father died, Joseph learned that his brothers were still afraid and suspicious that he might hold a grudge against them. When Joseph found out how they felt, the Bible says that he wept. Commentators differ in their interpretation of why Joseph cried, but he was sad for his brothers, who just didn't get it. They couldn't comprehend that Joseph could forgive them. They didn't have the same intimate trust in God, so they were not able to identify with Joseph's humble, forgiving response to the hurts for which they were responsible. So Joseph wept for his brothers who walked in fear of him because they could not see clearly through spiritual eyes.

Once again Joseph reassured them, telling them not to be afraid. He didn't sugarcoat the truth. He said, "You meant evil against me, but God meant it for good" (Gen 50:20, NASB).

Summing It Up

It's interesting how God weaves together the events of our lives and the events of the world in which we live. It's kind of like the weaving of an intricate tapestry. Thread by thread, a beautiful, detailed design unfolds. And that's what happened with Joseph. If we knew him today, he'd be one of those people who would cause us to shake our heads and say, "Bad luck just seems to follow that guy!" But God was doing a deliberate work through Joseph that ultimately executed a divine purpose through his human pain.

I want you to stop for a moment and think about any situation that might be causing you to struggle with bitter resentment. If it's loneliness, can you see that God is using your isolation to draw you more intimately to Him? If you battle a life-threatening illness, is your spirit growing healthier and more alive than ever? Whatever your circumstances, are you able to say, as Joseph did, that God intended it for good? Are you able to really believe that He is able to make your pain purposeful?

If not, here are five principles from Joseph's story that you can practice to help you deal with resentment.

Anti-resentment Principle #1: Acceptance

The first choice you can make when you find yourself in a state of resentment over an unfair situation is to ask God for the grace and patience to accept the situation. Acknowledge that He can use the circumstance to bring about good in your life, and ask Him to fill you with the character of Jesus. Please don't think that what I'm suggesting is an "easy fix." It's a tough challenge to make this choice. Circumstances like these are the crucible—the firing process that God uses to refine and mold us into His image.

As I understand it, a silversmith knows that the impurities have been purged out of the silver when he is able to see his own image reflected in the boiling liquid metal. The same is true with God. When

He looks down into the fire of injustice in our lives and sees His image finally shining through us, He knows that the impurities in our character have been cauterized.

So tough as it seems, don't fight the fire. Remember Keith and Mary Korstjens, and be challenged by their example. Submit to the fiery trial—even embrace it—and God will use it to brand His character into you.

Anti-resentment Principle #2: Play Offense

When someone hurts you—when life deals you mud—the natural response is to become defensive. But the right response is to play offense. The apostle Paul encourages us not to be overcome by evil, but rather to overcome evil with good (Rom 12:21). This may mean that instead of fighting back in a conflict, we turn the other cheek and maybe even go so far as to do something that will bless the offender. We may have to surrender our right to be in control, even though we have a right to be. The only possible way to do this is to cooperate with God, and when we do He will use our pain for a purpose that may draw others to Him in the process.

Anti-resentment Principle #3: Look through Other Eyes

A third "resentment buster" is to get out of yourself and look through the eyes of your offender. Again, this is not an easy thing to do, especially when you feel abused and mistreated. But, with God's help, it is possible and it will provide tremendous liberating insight.

Let me paint you a hypothetical picture. Say you are behind someone in heavy traffic and his car slows to an annoying speed. As the car creeps along, you become more and more angry. You may even go so far as to shake your fist or let your irritation show in some other way.

Maybe this person is just a pokey driver, in which case your irritation is justified. In fact, driving too slow can actually cause an accident. But what if the driver has suddenly and unexpectedly become dizzy or sick? If you were to learn this information, your irritation would immediately change to concern and compassion.

This is what is called a "paradigm" shift—a major change in how we see things. It happens when we receive input from another point of view that causes us to change our perspective. When we are able to see things through another person's eyes, one of two things will happen. We might realize that we were wrong about someone and that we are the ones who need to ask for forgiveness. Or we might get some new insight that will make us compassionate toward the other person or people. Either way, we feel less like a victim and find it easier to implement a vertical response.

Paul advises us to do everything we can to live at peace with others (Rom 12:18). Once we have put ourselves in the other person's shoes, we are freed to make peace with them. And then the ball is in their court. If they don't respond in kind, we can freely move on, released from resentment's grip.

Anti-resentment Principle #4: Be Teachable
A fourth step we can take as a safeguard against bitterness is to be open and searching for God's lessons. These lessons, learned through trial, are like seeds of rejoicing in our lives that keep us rooted and grounded in the Lord.

You know, "happiness" is not the same as "joy." Happiness is a transient feeling that tags along with good times. It's a fleeting imitation of joy, which is a deeper emotion that abides through both good times and bad. True joy comes as a result of connection with God and will not melt away in a fiery trial—if we choose a vertical response. Paul speaks with satisfaction of how he "learned to be content whatever the circumstances" (Phil 4:11). If we are teachable like Paul, we can enjoy that satisfying feeling of contentment in even the most trying times, and our inner joy will shine out as a testimony for Jesus Christ.

Anti-resentment Principle #5: The Golden Rule

There is one last tried-and-true action we can take into our battle with resentment. It's so universally accepted that it's become known, even among unbelievers, as "the golden rule." It simply means to treat others as we would want to be treated, and when we practice this principle, it's a win-win situation. There is something very healing about being kind to someone who has hurt us. It gives us a feeling of taking control, and it models the character of Christ. Acts of kindness can slowly build a bridge in a bad relationship, sometimes resulting in complete healing and even friendship. Once again, our individual responsibility is to do our part at being peacemakers. Doing so does not guarantee a positive response from another person, but it does free us from being a victim and allows us to move on with a clear conscience.

Once again you may be shaking your head and thinking, "How on earth can I do this? Maybe I can practice the golden rule in little things, but I don't have it within me to apply this principle to the really hard hurts in my life." And once again, I say that the key is submission to the lordship of Jesus. He's the ultimate expert on forgiveness. He has experienced our hurts and many more besides.

We are told that Jesus "had to be made like His brothers in every way, in order that He might become a merciful and faithful high priest in service to God, and that He might make atonement for the sins of the people" (Heb 2:17). No one in the history of the world has been treated more unjustly than Jesus Christ was when He hung on a cross—stripped, beaten, and mocked. But God gave purpose to the pain endured by His Son and used it as a vessel of reconciliation. Then He came into our hearts to help us deal with every possible hurt we can imagine.

The Bottom Line

Ponder the following interesting story, which dramatically sets the stage for the dark final hour of history.

At the end of time, billions of people were scattered on a great plain before God's throne. Some of the groups near the front talked heatedly—not with cringing shame, but with belligerence.

"How can God judge us? How can He know about suffering?"

The brunette jerked back a sleeve to reveal a tattooed number from a Nazi concentration camp. "We endured terror, beatings, torture, death."

In another group, a black man lowered his collar, showing an ugly rope burn. "Lynched for no crime but being black. We have suffocated in slave ships, been wrenched from loved ones, toiled till only death gave release."

Far out across the plain were hundreds of such groups. Each had a complaint against God for the evil and suffering He permitted in this, His world.

"How lucky God is to live in Heaven where all is sweetness and light, where there (was) no weeping, no fear, no hunger, no hatred."

"Indeed, what does God know about what man has been forced to endure in this world?"

"After all, God leads a pretty sheltered life."

So each group sent out a leader, chosen because he had suffered the most. There was a Jew, a black, an untouchable from India, an illegitimate, a person from Hiroshima, and one from a Siberian slave camp. In the center of the plain they consulted with each other. At last they were ready to present their case. It was rather simple: Before God would be qualified to be their judge, He must endure what they had endured. Their decision was that God should be sentenced to live on Earth—as a man.

But, because He was God, they set certain safeguards to be sure He could not use His divine powers to help Himself:

Let Him be born a Jew.

Let the legitimacy of His birth be doubted, so that none will know who is really His father.

Let Him champion a cause so just, but so radical, that it brings down upon Him the hate, condemnation, and eliminating efforts of every major traditional and established religious authority.

Let Him try to describe what no man has ever seen, tasted, heard, or smelled. Let Him try to communicate God to men.

Let Him be betrayed by His dearest friends.

Let Him be indicted on false charges, tried before a prejudiced jury, and convicted by a cowardly judge.

Let Him see what it is to be terribly alone and completely abandoned by every living thing.

Let Him be tortured and let Him die. Let Him die the most humiliating death—with common thieves.

As each leader announced his portion of the sentence, loud murmurs of approval went up from the great throng of people. When the last had finished pronouncing sentence, there was a long silence. No one uttered another word. No one moved—for suddenly all knew . . .God had already served His sentence.[2]



ॐ   ॐ   ॐ

Have you accepted this gift of redemption from the One who secured it for you through His own intense and undeserved suffering? Is a root of bitterness eating away at you and keeping you from the joy of reconciled fellowship with others and with God?

If your answer to these questions is "yes," will you go before His throne right now and give Him your bitter accusations and resentful attitude? He is waiting to administer the antidote that transforms your pain into promise and gives you His everlasting joy.

Applying the Antidote

A foolproof treatment for resentment is found in Rom 8:28: "And we know that in all things God works for the good of those who love him, who have been called according to his purpose." Notice that there is no disclaimer. It doesn't say God works for good in "some things"; it says "all things!" But you must swallow the whole pill. God works everything for good for those who have responded to His call. Is that you? If so, this verse is for you.

If you have a computer, sit down, choose an interesting font, select an oversized type and make a sign, inserting your name in Rom 8:28. (If you don't have a computer, good old-fashioned pen and paper will do.) Keep your personalized promise in a place where you will look at it often. When you are feeling resentful or bitter, claim this verse as your own. Here's an example:

I, Glenn, know that in EVERYTHING (yes, every single thing) God works for my good. Why? Because I love Him and am willing to cooperate with His plan for my life.

For: Resentment

"Even as Christ forgave you, so you also must do."

—Col 3:12 (NKJV)

Chapter 10

Toxic Temptation

Temptation: The enticement to commit an unwise or immoral act, especially by promise of reward.

—THE AMERICAN
HERITAGE DICTIONARY
OF THE ENGLISH LANGUAGE

MARK ANTONY, the famous Roman statesman, was a very gifted man. History heralds him as being a man of superior intelligence, a strong leader, and a courageous soldier. He had many fine attributes to his credit, plus one major flaw: He was weak.

On the outside, Mark Antony was impressive and magnificent. But inside, he was self-indulgent and vulnerable to temptation. Mark Antony's best-known temptation also proved to be the most costly. Her name was Cleopatra. She was a beautiful, exotic queen who sailed on a river barge from Egypt to Rome—and right into Mark Antony's heart. For centuries, their adulterous relationship has been the subject of literature, theater, and movie scripts. It was a passionate and undisciplined relationship that cost Mark Antony his wife, his power as a world leader, and, ultimately, his life.

One tragic day, Cleopatra manipulated him into believing that she was dead. Beside himself, the powerful leader fell on his own sword and took his life. He died because of his addiction to a destructive relationship that was once a temptation—one that could have, and should have, been avoided.

Temptation is one of life's most deadly toxins. Every one of us has a little set of scales inside. When temptation comes, we weigh the consequences on those scales and make a choice. I'm sure that we all want to do the wise and prudent thing—to make the moral choice. But temptation entices us to take a shortcut and to seize something that is irresistible to us, without first seeking, and then waiting for, God's will.

Has this ever happened to you? You want something so badly, and you want it now. Maybe it is even something good, something God intends to give you, in His time. But you just can't wait, so you seize it.

Temptation entices us away from God's will and attracts us toward our own will. The sad thing is that, although we might revel in the object of our temptation, it will be only temporary if we circumvent God. Eventually, the pain of giving in to temptation will spoil the temporary pleasure.

Not all of us face such major temptations as Mark Antony's adultery, but none of us avoid temptation altogether. In fact, it may be the little things that lure us that are the most dangerous because they seem so minor and petty. Like an iceberg hidden beneath the waters of the sea, they can cause a sudden, tragic shipwreck in our lives.

What are the things that tempt you? Are you prone to stretch the truth a bit to suit your purpose? Do you fight an irresistible urge to gossip? Are you resistant to spending time in daily prayer and Bible study because of activities—even good ones—that draw you away from God? Have you ever been tempted to commit a sexual sin? Have you ever yielded to that temptation?

Whatever temptations lure you, the Bible offers help to reject them and to live the victorious life He desires for you.

Three Muscle Builders

James outlines three principles to help strengthen our will against temptation. He tells us, "When tempted, no one should say, 'God is tempting me.' For God cannot be tempted by evil, nor does He tempt anyone" (Jas 1:13).

James uses the word "when" and not the word "if." This suggests that everyone encounters temptation. We aren't any different than the next person, yet sometimes Satan will confuse our thinking by making us feel guilty about being tempted—as if we are to blame. We must remember that we cannot avoid temptation, and it's not sin until we give in to it.

Martin Luther gave an illustration of this principle. He pointed out that you can't stop a bird from flying over your head, but you can stop it from building a nest in your hair. There's a nugget of great advice in this illustration. We should not allow ourselves to be filled with anxiety or a false sense of guilt when we are tempted because our sin nature predisposes us to a battle with temptation. Simply accepting this gives us the upper hand. But we can make sure that temptation does not control us and does not make it easy to rationalize doing something that is immoral or unwise.

A second muscle builder from James is the assurance that temptation does not come from God. He says, "God cannot be tempted by evil, nor does He tempt anyone" (Jas 1:13).

God is righteous and holy. Yet, ever since the Garden of Eden, men and women have tried to blame their own weaknesses on God. What did Adam say when God confronted him about his sin of disobedience? Something like, "Eve did it! I was just minding my own business here in the Garden, being a good guy and doing the right things. Then You had to complicate things by bringing that woman into my life and causing me to sin." Adam blamed Eve directly, and he also implied that it was God's fault because He created Eve. But

God does not tempt anyone, and we must avoid blaming our own weakness on Him.

If temptation doesn't come from God, where does it come from? In 1 John, we learn about three sources: the world, the flesh, and Satan. We live in a sinful, fallen world where we can expect to bump into temptation over and over again. And since we are, by nature, people "of the flesh," we will be attracted to the world's temptation like metal to a magnet. Finally, Satan will be in that world, trying to entice us to give in. You can count on it. The late comedian Flip Wilson was famous for his line, "The devil made me do it." He was zeroing in on a human tendency to blame our weaknesses and failings on Satan, but the truth is that Satan cannot make us do anything. He can, however, tempt us.

A third principle about temptation is that it usually follows a pattern. As James points out, "each one is tempted when, by his own evil desire, he is dragged away and enticed. Then, after desire has conceived, it gives birth to sin, and sin, when it is full grown, gives birth to death" (Jas 1:14–15).

You can see from these verses that there is a definite four-stage pattern to the downward spiral into temptation.

Stage 1: The Bait Is Planted

Interestingly enough, in the original Greek, the word translated as "enticed" is a fishing term. Fishermen know that it is a science to use just the right bait for a particular fish. Nobody ever caught a fish by strapping a light bulb to a line and dropping it in the water, but the right kind of bait will lure a fish to bite right into that hook.

Satan uses this strategy, too. He looks for just the right bait to lure us as individuals. What entices me is not the same bait that entices you. Each of us is unique, so Satan goes to great lengths to discover our areas of weakness, then he hangs them right out there in front of us.

Stage 2: Lured by the Bait

The next stage is when we give ourselves permission to "desire" the bait. Because of our sin nature, we are inevitably drawn to the lure. But let me emphasize that, even at this stage, no sin has been committed. Our desires are just a part of daily life, and we should not entertain false guilt over the first two stages of temptation.

Stage 3: Giving In

Sin does occur, however, when desire meets temptation and causes us to give in. This is not something that just happens to us. It is a choice of our will. The Bible assures us that "there hath no temptation taken you but such that is common to man, but God is faithful and will, with the temptation, provide a way of escape" (1 Cor 10:13). The key to victory against temptation lies in staying close to God. When we deliberately choose to cooperate with God, He will then give the victory.

Sadly, the reverse is also true. That is, when we choose to rely on our own will, we must expect to be "hooked" by Satan's bait. This is the third stage—the "giving in." Again we can apply the fishing analogy. When a fish is swimming in the shallows of a lake and suddenly spots that attractive bait, he has to make a choice. It's a simple choice: to bite or not to bite. If the fish bites, it's over. And if you choose to bite a tempting lure, you are a goner, too.

Stage 4: A Tragic End

The final stage of temptation's trap is the result that it produces in our lives. Unfortunately, this is where the fish analogy fails to apply. For a fish who bites, the end comes pretty quickly. The moment he takes the bait he feels that hook, and within a short time the fish dies.

But in life, the "hook" may remain hidden for days, weeks, and maybe even years. Whenever we yield to temptation—no matter how small—there will be a loss in our life.

Scott suffered the most tragic loss imaginable when he gave in to temptation. Scott was a pastor of a large church with a radio and television ministry that reached thousands, an author of inspirational books that changed people's lives, a teacher of God's Word, a devoted husband and loving father—he had it all. He was a bright light for Christ in his community.

Scott's descent into darkness began innocently enough. What could possibly be wrong about cultivating a friendship with Joanne—a young, attractive member of his ministry team. Scott and Joanne didn't start their friendship thinking it would lead them into sexual sin. In fact, they believed that their love for Christ would protect them from falling into such a trap. Mistake number one.

Mistake number two came when they rationalized that it was perfectly legitimate to have lunch together on an occasional basis. Occasionally turned into regularly, and pretty soon Scott and Joanne also found justification to work late without other staff members around. Mistake number three—and counting.

You know the rest of the story. Lust swept Scott and Joanne into the sexual sin of adultery, and at first it seemed so right. But eventually their secret affair became a public matter that ended Scott's marriage and split his church apart. The man who was once such a bright, spiritual light in his community was now pointed to as an example of hypocrisy. After it was all over, Scott's heart broke to realize that, because he yielded to temptation, Jesus—his gracious Lord—was shamed and discredited.

The story I've shared is a fictional one, based on details from several stories that are sadly true. What's most sobering about it is that this could happen to me or to you just as easily as it happened to Scott. We cannot rely on our Christianity to make us immune to temptation, no matter what our area of weakness. And we can't escape the consequence of giving in. It may be a subtle one—a slight loss of integrity or a loss of credibility—or it may be a huge loss, as was the case in Scott's story. The point is that giving in to temptation will always come back to bite us.

How to Turn Temptation into Triumph

As we've already seen, temptation is inevitable, but not unbeatable. As Christians, we have the Holy Spirit to help us resist and prayer to keep us close to God. We also have His specific instructions and promises to which we can go every day through Bible study—words that are powerful in their ability to conform us to His righteous character. We have all the tools to resist temptation, but we need a strategy for using them. Let me give you five practical tips to help turn temptation into triumph.

Run, Run, Run!

As a general rule, the best way to deal with a problem is to confront it, but with temptation it is best to keep your distance.

I once heard a story about a man who had a pet boa constrictor. When he first got the snake, it was just a baby, and the man would take the reptile out of its cage every day and play with it. As the snake grew, it got bigger and stronger until it was monstrous. Still, the man would take it out for play, until one day the boa constrictor did what this particular species of snake is famous for doing: It wrapped around the man and strangled the life out of him.

To me, this is symbolic of how a seemingly harmless temptation can grow, almost imperceptibly, until we are caught in its lethal grip. We can get so accustomed to living with it that we are unprepared for the inevitable moment when it strangles us.

To put this in a more personal framework, let me ask you some questions:

Are there certain places you should avoid going—or people you should avoid seeing?

Do you have a weakness for books, magazines, television shows, or movies that are immoral in content or so visually stimulating that they cause you to think impure thoughts or commit ungodly acts?

Does your tendency to gossip stir up trouble and cause harm to others?

Are you living in fear that you'll get caught next time you fudge on your tax return?

Do you have a secret addiction that needs to be addressed—alcohol, prescription drugs, or maybe gambling?

Be honest, and if you answer "yes" to even one of these questions, you should avoid those people, places, and things that stir up desires or lusts. The Bible tells us that, if possible, we should run from temptation. If we don't, we should not be surprised to find ourselves in a mess.

Be Ready to Fight

What about those times, though, when it's impossible to run? We are human, after all, and we don't have the ability to see ahead. We can't always anticipate when temptation will lunge at us, or the form it will take. That's why it is essential that we always be spiritually armed.

I have good friends who love to play golf, and they tell me that it's a real art to pick the right club for each type of shot. It's the same way with temptation. We need to pick the right weapon for our individual weak points.

For example, in regard to sexual sin, the best weapon is avoidance. Joseph ran from a seductive woman, and we should, too. That may mean turning off the television, throwing a magazine into a dumpster, or getting up and leaving a movie theater, even though you've paid a small fortune to see a film. Running away, in this case, is not the cowardly thing to do; it's the courageous thing to do.

Perhaps you're vulnerable to the lure of material things. You spend your paycheck before it's in the bank and you never seem to have anything to give to others or to the Lord's work. In this case, your defense might be learning how to plan ahead. You might even want to arrange for a determined amount of each paycheck to be transferred automatically to a ministry fund or a special savings account that is set aside for God.

Perhaps jealousy is your personal area of weakness. When tempted to think vicious, bitter thoughts or engage in gossip about a person, your strategy might involve getting alone and praying for that person instead. It's amazing how prayer for someone will release us from the grip of jealousy and resentment.

Through these examples, you can see how the best defense is a practical offense. Take a good look at yourself and identify the areas of weakness in your own life, then find your weapon—and use it!

Visualize the Future

Another practical measure is to think through the consequences of giving in to temptation. Set your desires aside and remind yourself of the ultimate pain that will erase the temporary pleasure if you give in. Imagine what would happen if one of those fish we were talking about earlier could attend an educational seminar. After viewing a video of the hook inside the bait and of other fish flopping around in a boat, gasping for air, and being gutted for someone's dinner, I doubt that any self-respecting fish would go after that particular bait again. I know this is a ludicrous example, but sometimes a silly image can remind us of lessons we need to apply in our lives, and I hope this one will come back to you again and again when you are tempted. Constantly remind yourself that pain will ultimately replace pleasure if you say "yes" to any temptation, small or great.

Moses is a good example of someone who chose to renounce short-term pleasure in favor of long-term blessings. Moses was adopted and raised by a member of Egypt's royalty. As an adult, he could have chosen to remain part of that privileged circle, but Moses knew it would not afford him any eternal benefits. We are told that he chose instead to be mistreated with God's people, rather than enjoy the pleasures of pagan society for a brief time (Heb 11:24–29).

Garbage In, Garbage Out

Another action we can take is to saturate our minds with God's Word. The saying "garbage in, garbage out" means that if we fill our minds with junk, it will also flow out of us. The reverse is also true. If we "take in" God's Word, then His righteousness will flow out of our hearts and keep us standing firm. The psalmist says:

> How can a young man keep his way pure? By living according to Your word. I seek you with all my heart; do not let me stray from your commands. I have hidden your word in my heart that I might not sin against you. (Ps 119:9–11)

If you are not regularly reading and studying God's Word, then you are battling temptation with a crippling handicap. I urge you to make a practice of opening the Bible and "ingesting" scripture every day. This practice is just as essential to growing strong spiritually as food is for the growth of a healthy body. Being involved in a regular Bible study group or a Sunday school class is an excellent preventative measure. You need a place where you can experience face-to-face encouragement with people who will hold you accountable.

Once in a While Doesn't Cut It

What would happen if you rarely brushed your teeth? Eventually decay would eat them away, and you'd constantly be in pain. The best way to fight tooth decay is to establish a lifelong habit of daily dental hygiene.

Think of temptation in a similar way. Since temptation is an ever-present threat to our spiritual well-being, the best way is to be on guard and take preventative measures every day. A few simple, spiritual habits practiced on a daily basis can safeguard us against the tragic consequence of biting the bait.

One of the things I'm most looking forward to about being in heaven is that this wrestling match with temptation will be over. Just like everyone else, I can't wait to see the streets of gold and my mansion in the sky. But most of all, I'm longing to be able to rise in the morning and do what I feel like doing, because whatever that is will be perfectly in tune with God's will. Won't it be glorious not to have to analyze everything?

It All Adds Up

How are you doing in your battle against temptation? Are you prepared for the battle, or have you neglected to protect yourself from the enemy? Are you strong when it comes to the "biggies," but weak and vulnerable to the less obvious, more sinister traps of life?

It's the little things that eventually add up to make the sum total of our lives. If you ever had to make a choice between following Jesus or being put to death, what would you do? I guarantee that your decision would depend on the daily choices you've made that have either formed you into a strong, durable witness or a weak, vulnerable coward.

C. S. Lewis's famous *Screwtape Letters* has an interesting scene. Screwtape, who typifies Satan, says to Wormwood, his young charge:

*My dear Wormwood, obviously you are making excellent prog-
ress. My only fear is lest in attempting to hurry the patient you
awaken him to a sense of his real position. For you and I, who see
that position as it really is, must never forget how totally different it ought to appear to him. We know that we have introduced
a change of direction in his course which is already carrying him
out of his orbit around the Enemy: (God) but he must be made
to imagine that all the choices which have effected this change
of course are trivial and revocable. He must not be allowed to
suspect that he is now, however slowly, heading right away from
the sun on a line which will carry him into the cold and dark of
utmost space.[1]*

What choices have you made? Have they changed your spiritual orbit? Have you slowly, almost imperceptibly, become anaesthetized
by Satan, who is luring you into the downward spiral of temptation?
Jesus is the way out of the cold dark spiral and into God's warm
Light. Call out to Him today and ask Him to turn temptation's trap
into triumph.

Applying the Antidote

The best defense against temptation is a daily offensive of prayer and Bible study. Here's an exercise to help get you started:

Make a commitment to get up ten minutes earlier every day for two weeks. Ask someone to hold you accountable. When you arise, go to a special, quiet spot. Pray out loud, asking God to:

- Reveal your personal areas of weakness.
- Show you specific ways to avoid them.
- Give you scriptural "weapons" to use against them.
- Replace your particular weaknesses with His strength. (Be specific.)

After two weeks, you will want to continue this spiritual habit—God's antidote for toxic temptation.

For: Temptation

"No temptation has seized you except what is common to man. And God is faithful; he will not let you be tempted beyond what you can bear. But when you are tempted, he will also provide a way out so that you can stand up under it."

—1 Cor 10:13 (NIV)

Toxic Depression

THE OWNERS OF A parakeet were attempting to clean their pet's cage one day by probing the cage floor with the hose of their vacuum cleaner. To their horror, the little bird got sucked into the vacuum. In a panic, they quickly disassembled the machine and found their pet inside the vacuum bag—trembling with fear but still alive. In an attempt to revive the little bird, they doused it with water and blasted it with hot air from a hair dryer. Several weeks later, a friend asked how the parakeet was doing. "He's fine," they replied, "but he doesn't sing much any more."

Perhaps you can identify with that poor traumatized bird. You've been through some very tough times. From the outside, you look just fine, but deep down you know you have some traumatic scars. You have the blues, and you don't feel like singing much any more.

Depression can take several forms—from mildly "down in the dumps" to a very serious condition known as clinical depression. Like all of the other spiritual toxins we've discussed, depression in any form can prevent us from living the joy-filled life God desires for us.

We need some biblical tools for dealing with depression. But before we proceed, let me issue a word of caution. I will be focusing on common types of transient depression that hit us all from time to time. If you find yourself in a daily state of emotional darkness—as though trapped in a tunnel with no light to show the way out—you need a type of help that will not be offered in this book. I strongly encourage you to get that help from a committed Christian counselor.

In fact, if you are in a state of clinical depression, it could be a matter of life or death. In this case, the most spiritual decision you can make today may not be to spend more time in prayer or in reading scripture. The most responsible choice may be to seek help from a clinical psychologist or even a medical doctor. There are many fine professionals who have been called by God to a ministry of counseling. As the poet John Donne wrote, "No man is an island," and God did not intend for us to bear our heaviest burdens all by ourselves.

Unfortunately, many Christians are reluctant to seek counseling for several reasons. For some, there is a perceived negative stigma associated with psychological counseling so they simply deny their need. Others wrestle with guilt because they have concluded that it's not "spiritual" to be depressed. They convince themselves that they are not good Christians, since God has given them so much to enjoy and be thankful for, and yet they are depressed. Outwardly they deny the inner torment that pulls them into a pit of despair. This is a tragedy, since God understands our emotional makeup and all the factors that contribute to depression. He is pleased when we acknowledge it and deal with it—and our denial must frustrate Him.

Singin' the Blues

Thankfully, most of us never experience the kind of depression I just described. But transient depression—"the blues"—is a common condition that all of us pass through occasionally. Several root causes will be touched on here.

Physiological Causes

Feelings of depression can have a physiological base. There may be a medical reason—a chemical imbalance or a reaction to a prescription drug. When we don't take proper care of our body and give it adequate nourishment, rest, and exercise, we leave ourselves vulnerable to a corresponding breakdown in our emotional and mental states. We become tired and downhearted.

The great revivalist Robert Murray McShane (1814–1843) was a gifted young preacher who could really move a crowd. But he was so consumed by his calling that he neglected to take care of himself. He became exhausted and burned out—so much so that his health began to fail.

Finally, he died before his fortieth birthday. Historians say about 100,000 people lined the streets on the day of his funeral. During his brief ministry, he had had a positive impact on so many people—who knows how many more he might have brought to Jesus if he had lived a normal lifespan? It is said that on his death bed McShane pondered that very thought. Before he died, he is reported to have said, "God gave me a message, and I've gone and killed the horse that carried it."

I tell you this story to caution you to care for your body, mind, and spirit. God has given you a reason to be alive, just as He gave one to Robert Murray McShane. God has carefully positioned you on this earth and given you a message to share with those within your sphere of influence. Part of the responsibility He hands to you is to take care of yourself so that you don't break down physically or burn out mentally before you have a chance to complete His plan.

Psychological Causes

Studies indicate that depression can also be related to psychological issues dating back to our earliest experiences. Dr. Clyde Narramore explains that, in order to grow emotionally healthy and confident, every human being needs to feel affirmed, secure, and happy.[1] When parents fail to display interest and affection, their child begins to feel rejected, unloved, and unworthy—dark feelings he or she can internalize for life.

Seeds of self-doubt and low self-esteem can also be planted in children when their parents' style of discipline is harsh and demeaning, or when they are compared unfavorably to their siblings or friends. And when parents are overly critical or hold to an impossible standard of perfection, they set up their child to wrestle with depression later in life.

Spiritual Causes

Spiritual issues also trigger bouts of depression. I personally believe that we sometimes suffer from depression because sin alienates us from God. It is unlikely that Adam and Eve were depressed before the great fall in the Garden of Eden. Prior to their rebellious first acts of sin, they were in a very intimate, close relationship with their Creator—one that was severed in an instant when Eve disobeyed God. We were created to be in relationship with Him, and when we're not, we feel depressed and incomplete.

My son John once had to have surgery (he has actually had thirty surgeries, but is healthy and active today). This particular time, we became very worried because he was obviously depressed in the hospital. A nurse assured us that "hospital blues" are very normal, especially with children, because they are separated from family and friends and are away from the secure home environment. We saw how true this is when we brought John home and he snapped out of his depressed state. To me, this is a picture of humanity. We are born into a state of sin that alienates us from our Father and removes us from the security of His kingdom. Unless we are reconciled through Jesus Christ, we will suffer from an aching spiritual depression all our life. But when we "come home" to Him we feel secure, and as we grow in our relationship with Him the depression lifts. So the very first step to breaking free of depression is to take that step of faith and receive Jesus.

Even after we come to Christ, our relationship can often be marred through acts of self-willed disobedience. With God, living "my way" just doesn't cut it. In order to enjoy a satisfying relationship that frees our soul from darkness, we must deliberately ask Him on a daily basis to be in control. How wonderful it will be when we are in heaven with Him—a place where depression will be nonexistent. What joy we look forward to when we are intimate with our Maker in the way Adam and Eve were before the fall. In the meantime, however, we cannot hope to reach a state of sinless perfection. We need to apply daily doses of repentance to prevent spiritual depression from overwhelming us.

Two Biblical Comrades

If you are familiar with the Bible, you already know it is full of stories about people who struggled with problems and issues, just like you and I do. Two of those were Moses and Elijah—mighty men of God who were prone to frequent feelings of depression.

Moses

What do you think about when someone mentions Moses? Do you envision him as the bold, mighty leader portrayed in the classic movie *The Ten Commandments* or the contemporary *Prince of Egypt*—the man who led God's people out of bondage in Egypt? Do you see a vision of the Red Sea parting before him to allow the people to escape from Pharaoh's chariot brigade? Moses was indeed a great and fearless leader who loved and trusted God, but he often battled "the blues."

As a student of the Bible, I've observed that most of the men and women who are mentioned, including Moses, struggled with depression. God chose to feature their stories in His Word so we can relate to real people and apply the lessons they learned to our daily life. God uses imperfect people like us.

Moses is a good example. Credited with writing the first five books of the Bible and leading the Israelites to the Promised Land, Moses is one of history's most impressive people. Yet overcommitment and an inferiority complex spoiled many successful ventures for him.

In his role as spiritual leader, Moses grew increasingly disappointed and angry with his people because they were behaving in a way that angered God. Scripture tells us that "The Lord became exceedingly angry, and Moses was troubled" (Num 11:10). In the original Hebrew, the connotation in this passage is that Moses was depressed.

What follows is a revelation of the comfortable, intimate friendship Moses had with God. Because he was spiritually secure, he felt free to vent his frustrations: "Why have You brought this trouble on your servant? What have I done to displease You that You have put the burden of all these people on me?" (Num 11:11)

Poor Moses was exasperated with the burden of leading a multitude of people who behaved like rebellious children and looked to him to meet their every need. He knew it wasn't God's fault that he was tired and worn out. He also knew he was perfectly free to pour his heart out to God. Here we see one of the most important antidotes for depression: prayer. Through prayer we can release our desperate feelings to God and receive His comfort and encouragement. And, of course, the more familiar we are with Him on a regular basis, the more personally comforted we will feel when we run to Him on a very bad day. As with any human relationship, if we want to feel free to ask God to listen to our troubles, we need to share our daily lives with Him as well.

You may recall that when God called Moses to lead His people, the response was not exactly an eager "Yes!" Instead, Moses argued with God, saying that he was inadequate for the job and that he was not good at public speaking. God was asking Moses to do a monumental job—a job that was too much for one man. But God knew Moses better than Moses knew himself, and so He did not waver. Moses was His man, and all He asked was that Moses be willing and available to let Him work through him.

The problem was that Moses perceived God's call to mean he had to be responsible for the people of Israel, not just to them. No wonder he was discouraged. He could not make the people respond to God's ways, and he felt like a failure when they did not. But God never expects us to assume responsibility for the way others respond to Him. He asks us to be examples and encouragers—to point them toward Him. Ultimately, no one can make another person believe.

I hope this will encourage you, whether you are a parent, a teacher, a team member, or whatever role you play in life. If we release the burden of other people's choices to the Lord, we will not so easily feel depressed or like a failure when their choices are wrong. Moses got into trouble when he looked out on a mob of rebellious, immature people and took their responsibility as his own.

Ironically, Moses allowed himself to become so busy doing things for God that he just didn't have any time to spend with God. Does that sound familiar to you? If you are too busy to sit down and talk to God, then you are too busy. And you can expect to be hit hard by depression if you don't take action to fend it off.

Jesus taught that His yoke is easy and His burden is light. If we are carrying a heavy burden, it must be because we are going over and beyond what God is calling us to do. Jesus taught us to be busy as we work for Him here on Earth. But He does not want us to be stressed out, angry, and spread thin.

To avoid all of these side effects, we must put spending time with God at the top of our list of priorities. Your schedule may be crammed to the limit, but if you come to God and say, "Lord, help me to see my schedule and my priorities through Your eyes," He will answer. He will reveal ways of budgeting your time so that you have the opportunity to be refreshed each day by His friendship. And I can promise you that if you put God first in your life, your time for other things will multiply and He will also show you ways to use whatever time you have more economically.

That's what He did for Moses, giving him very specific instructions:

> Bring me seventy of Israel's elders who are known to you as leaders and officials among the people. Have them come to the Tent of Meeting, that they may stand there with you. I will come down and speak with you there, and I will take the Spirit that is on you and put the Spirit on them. They will help you carry the burden of the people so that you will not have to carry it alone. (Num 11:16–17, NIV)

What a radical idea! Moses had never considered that God could—and would—use other people to help do the work. God called Moses to lead the people, and part of his responsibility was to involve them and delegate to them some of the tasks he was trying to do by himself.

Are you like Moses—depressed and miserable from overwork and self-doubt? If you are, ask Jesus to help you do two things. First, ask Him to help you formulate a "time budget" to help you give Him the place of top priority in your life that He deserves. Then, ask Him to take your burden—to be yoked together with you in everything you do. He will lift that burden and help you carry it successfully.

Elijah

Another great servant of God who suffered from depression was the prophet Elijah. Scripture shows how this spiritual warrior fell into a pit of despair that was so deep that it took him down for a while and had an impact on his physical and emotional health (1 Kings 19).

In general, it seems that depression comes on the heels of bad times—the death of a loved one, the breakup of a relationship, the loss of a job, or a time of sickness. But Elijah was a man who fell into depression after a time of success. He had just faced a group of cult leaders within the nation of Israel, and God vindicated him in a tremendously impressive way. And then came his fall:

> *Now Ahab told Jezebel everything Elijah had done and how he had killed all the prophets with the sword. So Jezebel sent a messenger to Elijah to say, "May the gods deal with me, be it ever so severely, if by this time tomorrow, I don't make your life like that of one of them." (1 Kgs 19:1–2, NIV)*

Elijah—the same man who had squared off with a crowd of cult priests—cowered in fear before this powerful, wicked queen. He was so frightened, in fact, that he literally ran for his life. Eventually he found himself in a desert, where he sat down and prayed that God would strike him dead.

Have you ever been there? So entangled in a cloud of depression that you truly wanted to die? In Elijah's case, there were three reasons for his depression.

First, he was physically exhausted. His face-off with the priests of Baal on Mount Carmel had wiped him out. Pastors refer to this type of exhaustion as the "blue Monday syndrome." The excitement of Sunday services is often followed by a post-adrenaline letdown. This is such a common experience in my life that Kimberly doesn't take me seriously on Mondays. She knows that anything I say on Monday will translate differently on Wednesday or Friday.

A second reason for Elijah's depression was that he was emotionally upset. He was being battered by criticism, even receiving death threats. Words can do great harm to people, as they did to Elijah. Hurt feelings and bitter resentment can drive people so far down that they want to die.

And finally, Elijah was faced with a spiritual crisis that ultimately manifested in a martyr complex. Feeling discouraged is something we can all relate to—a fact of life. But there is sometimes a tendency to overreact to those feelings and even to indulge ourselves in feelings of righteous indignation. We can act the part of a martyr, and that's what happened with Elijah.

Scripture gives us an encouraging account of how God dealt gently with Elijah during his personal crisis (1 Kings 19). There were several special ways God helped Elijah shed his depression—several antidotes you can incorporate into your own treatment plan.

First, God forced Elijah to address his physical need for rest and nourishment. He provided a comfortable spot for Elijah to sleep under the shade of a tree and sent an angel to guard him and even to wake him when it was time to eat. How practical and what a good example for us to follow when we, too, have become exhausted and depressed. A good night's sleep and a hearty breakfast can do wonders. It's not being self-indulgent to take care of yourself.

Then, after Elijah rested, God gave him a chance to talk about his depression. The almighty Counselor came to Elijah personally and asked, "What are you doing here, Elijah?" (1 Kgs 19:9) That's all the invitation Elijah needed to empty his heart, pouring out all the feelings he had stuffed inside himself.

God listened until the last word. Then, in an awesome way, He reminded the weary man about Whom he was talking to. He instructed him to "Go out and stand on the mountain in the presence of the Lord, for the Lord is about to pass by" (1 Kgs 19:11). As Elijah stood there, God came near—first in a mighty wind, then in a flaming fire, and finally in a powerful earthquake. All His might and power were on display. And then God spoke to Elijah through a still, small inner voice.

In this one encounter, God reminded Elijah through an impressive display that He is powerful enough to rule the forces of nature and personal enough to speak to us in the quiet places of our soul.

Sometimes when we are in the throes of depression, we forget that God is still on His throne.

After Elijah had rested for a while, God did something else for him. He sent him back to work. In 1 Kgs 19:15, Elijah receives his assignment: "Go back the way you came and go to the desert of Damascus. When you get there, anoint Hazail as King over Aram." God gave Elijah his time of rest—but He also called him back to action because work, especially for Him, is one of the best antidotes. He also gave him a good friend and companion named Elisha, who eventually was his successor in ministry.

And finally, after the darkness, God gave Elijah a new perspective. He showed him that he was not alone—seven thousand others in Israel had refused to give in to the idolatry that Elijah so hated. Even the greatest of challenges are a lot easier to deal with when we don't have to battle them by ourselves. Just knowing that others are going through the same things sheds a ray of hope and lifts the clouds of depression.

Purposeful Pain

Moses and Elijah would probably agree that their dark days were some of the most valuable days of their lives because they made the difference between knowing about God and really knowing God. In spite of their human weaknesses, both of these men truly desired nothing more than to be shaped into His holy image.

As with Moses and Elijah, God often uses the dog days of our lives to refine and fashion us—and to draw us closer to Him. So next time you find yourself in the wilderness, remember the lessons you have learned from these two mighty servants. Ask God to use your depression as a refiner's fire to make you a purer, stronger, and brighter witness for Him.

Applying the Antidote

Everyone gets "the blues," but chronic depression can be a deadly problem. To help you assess the magnitude of your own struggle, here is a short survey. If you answer "yes" to even one of these, I urge you to prayerfully seek out a qualified Christian therapist who will partner with God to set you free from toxic depression.

1. Is your depression constant rather than transient? Are you suffering for weeks and months, rather than an occasional difficult day?

2. Are you unable to function? Do you have trouble concentrating and performing even simple tasks? Have there been days when you simply could not get out of bed because of feelings of depression?

3. Do you feel so down that you have no energy or appetite?

4. Do you feel hopeless—not just occasionally, but all the time? Do you ever feel suicidal?

For: Depression

"Come to Me, all you who labor and are heavy laden, and I will give you rest."

—MATT 11:28 (NKJV)

Toxic
Fear

A Peanuts comic strip goes something like this: Good old neurotic Charlie Brown comes to Dr. Lucy's booth for therapy. Charlie is struggling with fear, and so Lucy asks him several questions in an attempt to get at the root of the problem.

"Do you have agoraphobia, the fear of open spaces?"

"No, that's not quite it," Charlie replies, shaking his big, round head.

"How about acrophobia, the fear of heights?" Lucy asks.

"No, that's not it either."

After several further futile inquiries, Lucy finally says, "Well, then, you just have panaphobia."

"What's that?" Charlie Brown asks hopefully.

"That's the fear of everything," she replies, tickled to death with her brilliant diagnosis.

"That's it," Charlie cries as though a miracle has happened. "That's it. That's what I've got."

Charlie Brown's life is like a mirror, reflecting back at us, in a humorous way, some of the bothersome traits and characteristics we see in ourselves. I can certainly identify with his free-floating paranoia, because I've experienced it. And I see it over and over again in people who come to me for counsel. Often, my effort to help is just about as effective as Lucy's diagnosis, because "fear" is a little word with a great big range of definitions that can be complex and elusive.

It's safe to say that fear is experienced by virtually every human being. Most of us would admit that generalized feelings of anxiety are part of everyday living in the world today. But it hasn't always been that way.

When God created Adam and Eve, He placed them in a totally safe environment. It was His intention to protect them forever from everything that could possibly harm them.

Just imagine. It must have been truly paradise to dwell in a beautiful, lush garden where the daily weather forecast was perfect and everything you could possibly need was close at hand. Imagine never having to be afraid of anything because God is personally guarding your home and meeting with you on a daily basis to make sure you are well, secure, and happy. That's the environment Adam and Eve lived in—until they made a choice to disobey God. Just one sinful decision upset everything and started a reign of death that continues in this world to this very day.

The First Death Sentence

There are countless verses in the Bible that talk about fear, beginning in the first book, Genesis. You may recall that, after his act of disobedience, Adam immediately hid from God. And when the Creator came looking for him, Adam explained that he was hiding because he was afraid.

Do you see the irony in this scene? Adam was hiding from the One who had provided a perfectly safe dwelling place. Adam's sin resulted in his becoming afraid of God, Who had previously protected and shielded him from every form of harm. Fear was the immediate consequence of sin—the foretaste of death that was the ultimate penalty for the first couple's rebellion.

Adam and Eve's sin did not affect just their own security. It put a wall of fear between God and every person who came after them. No longer would God walk and talk with His human children. The relationship became broken—or dysfunctional, to use a diagnostic word that has become popular in our time. We see an example in Exod 3:6, where Moses encountered God in a burning bush and became so terrified that he hid his face. We see another example when the children of Israel were learning to know and to trust God in their journey through the wilderness. On one occasion, Moses gathered them to meet with God at the base of Mount Sinai, and we are told that the people trembled with fear (Exod 19:16).

Fear still forms a barrier between God and people. The essence of the fear is anticipation of the death sentence God pronounced as the "wages" of sin. Have you ever thought about it that way? Because of sin, the whole human race has been condemned to death.

We're All in the Same Boat

Many fearful things are connected with death. We are in awe of it; it is an ominous unknown and we do not know what to expect, because from our vantage point it seems so final.

We also find death to be repugnant and unnatural, as illustrated by a story I once read about a fellow in Barcelona, Spain, who was driving a truck down the road with an empty casket in the back. Along the way, he picked up a hitchhiker who climbed into the flatbed of the truck where the casket was loaded.

Soon it began to rain, so the passenger opened the casket and climbed inside for shelter. Later, the driver stopped and picked up a few more travelers, who also piled into the back of the truck alongside the casket, not realizing a living, breathing person was inside. When the rain stopped, the casket lid opened and the man inside sat up and began to talk—much to the horror of the other passengers. In fact, they were so terrified that they all jumped off the moving truck and one of them was injured.

In spite of its unfortunate ending, this rather humorous story illustrates our instinctive horror of death. We want to escape from anything connected with it. We are afraid of dead people, and even more of "death" itself. In our minds the mere mention of death conjures up sinister images of foggy graveyards and the Grim Reaper. Yet, each of us has an inevitable appointment with death.

As we grow older, our anxiety over the prospect of dying becomes increasingly great. Usually by the time we hit midlife, it dawns on us that we really are mortal. This issue of man's mortality has been explored as a theme in many artistic works of literature, music, theater, and dramatic movies such as Fearless, My Life, and even more lighthearted films such as Sleepless in Seattle.

A Glimmer of Hope

It may be hard to believe, but fear of dying can have a very positive impact on an individual. I think of an article I once read about the famous boxer George Foreman. As you may know, Mr. Foreman is one of the all-time greats in the sport of boxing. In his youth, he won many championship matches, but what is even more impressive is that he made an amazing comeback at the age of forty-one when he challenged a much younger boxer named Evander Holyfield for the heavyweight championship of the world.

Mr. Foreman knew no fear when it came to entering the ring for a boxing match, but he was terrified of death. In fact, his fear of dying is what eventually motivated him to commit his life to Jesus Christ. Today, George Foreman is a pastor in Houston who devotes his life to ministering to people. But before he surrendered his life to Jesus, he tells of being consumed with a sinister desire to kill his opponents in the ring. All it would have taken to satisfy his bloodlust was just one guy—one life, taken in the ring.

What changed Mr. Foreman from a man who was afraid of dying into the man he is today—a man who preaches the gospel with an irresistible passion, kisses babies, jokes, and laughs? The transformation began with fear of terrible death—a fear that drove him to the foot of the Cross.

Putting Things into Perspective

Fear of death has, of course, motivated thousands of others like George Foreman to accept the life that Jesus offers. The reality is that death merits fearing; it is indeed a terrifying prospect.

A few years ago, *U.S. News & World Report* featured an article titled "The Rekindling of Hell."[1] The article reported that 60 percent of Americans believe in a literal place that is hell, but only 4 percent believe that they are in danger of being condemned to go there. People want to believe that there is a place where evil dictators, such as Saddam Hussein, or mass murderers, such as Jeffrey Dahmer, will get what they deserve. However, they don't want to believe that hell could be the eternal destination of an average, everyday person who is basically "good," according to human standards of behavior.

Paul reminds us that "all have sinned and fall short of the glory of God" (Rom 3:23). Everyone is a sinner—not just the Saddam Husseins and Jeffrey Dahmers. As Christians we know that "man is destined to die once and after that to face judgment" (Heb 9:27). Death is the natural consequence of sin, and we should all be afraid of it because—without exception—all of us deserve it, if we are judged according to our works or our personal worth. No matter how "good" we may be, we cannot earn a reprieve from the death sentence that was pronounced after the first sinful act of disobedience.

Let me offer an analogy. Imagine that the human race was going to participate in a long-jump competition across the Grand Canyon, which is about a mile across. Very few people—only athletes like Carl Lewis or Mike Powell—could jump twenty-nine or thirty feet, at most. Someone like me would leap five or ten feet, and others would make yet shorter jumps. Even Lewis or Powell couldn't look back and laugh at the rest of us for our inadequacy, because all of us would fall very short of jumping the breadth of the Grand Canyon.

Think of the spiritual heroes and heroines we admire so much. Even they fall short of God's holy standard. Ultimately, we must all acknowledge the truth of the sobering pronouncement that "the wages of sin is death" (Rom 6:23). Each one of us—no matter how rich or poor, how famous or infamous—will die one day and be sentenced at God's judgment seat to spend eternity either in heaven, with Him, or in hell, apart from Him. So the bad news is that death is real, and it is indeed something to be afraid of. But there is good news, too.

The Invasion of the Fearless One

The good news is that Jesus has conquered death on our behalf.

He is the Fearless One who came to earth as a human baby, just as we did. Then, after going through the same growth process and experiencing life here on earth, Jesus took everyone's death sentence to the Cross and, through His death and resurrection, broke down the barrier of sin that has separated us from God since the fall of Adam and Eve.

If you take a few minutes and read through the first few chapters of Luke, which record the birth of Jesus Christ, you might be amazed at how many "fear nots" you find. For example, when an angel came to tell Mary that she would bear God's son, she was told not to fear the scary unknowns she was facing. "Do not be afraid, Mary, you have found favor with God," is the assurance she received from the angelic messenger (Luke 1:30).

Later the Holy Spirit spoke through Zechariah, proclaiming the good news that Jesus was coming to free people from fear (Luke 1:74). And in the beloved scene that has been reenacted many times in children's Christmas pageants, the heavenly host of angels sang a song of good cheer as they directed the shepherds to Bethlehem, where they found the baby Jesus (Luke 2:8–14). He grew to be the Fearless One who came to pay our debt for sin and to forever set us free from bondage to fear.

There's a true story from the Great Depression that illustrates the compassion of Jesus' redemptive gift. At that time, New York City was governed by Mayor La Guardia, who regularly served as a judge in night court.

One evening, a very poor man was brought before him, charged with stealing a loaf of bread to feed his desperately hungry family. Mayor La Guardia was sworn to uphold the standard of the law, so he fined the man ten dollars for his crime—and then he did something that was remarkable. He left the judge's bench, walked over to the man and handed him a ten dollar bill from his own wallet, so that he could pay the fine and be set free.

What a human picture this paints of God's merciful act in paying for our sins in a way that was costly to Him. Sin is serious business to our perfectly righteous God. His standard of holiness requires death as the consequence, and so we have been sentenced to death.

But, through Jesus, God "left the judge's seat" and came to Earth to personally provide the payment for our debt of sin. God did His part to deal with toxic fear, and we must do ours. It isn't enough just to believe intellectually; we must accept His gift of salvation and surrender ourselves in personal commitment to Jesus.

On paper, that sounds pretty simple, doesn't it? But total surrender involves trust—the opposite of fear. And in our humanness, trust can be pretty hard.

You have probably heard the story about a famous tightrope performer named James Blondin who strung a rope across Niagara Falls for an exhibition. Before the eyes of an incredulous crowd, Blondin walked across that tightrope, with the falls crashing below. Then he did something even more daring. He went over the tightrope again, this time pushing a wheelbarrow across and back, to the further amazement of incredulous onlookers.

As the story goes, Blondin went over to a man who was one of the spectators and asked him if he believed what he had seen—that he really did walk across that tightrope. The man nodded that he believed. Then he asked the man if he believed he could push the wheelbarrow across and back with a man sitting in it, to which he also replied that he believed. But when he invited the man to get inside the wheelbarrow for a ride across the tightrope, the guy flatly refused. He believed with his mind, but he couldn't bring himself to trust James Blondin with his life.

Sometimes we're like that, too. We can evaluate the biblical and historical evidence and find it in ourselves to believe that Jesus lived, died, and rose again. To trust Jesus with our lives is much harder, but we must trust Jesus with and for our lives. Inside His wheelbarrow, we are as safe as a baby cradled in a mother's arms, no matter what dangers are rushing around and beneath us.

The Power of Fearlessness

When we really trust in Jesus and ask Him to take charge of our lives, His Spirit within us imparts a liberating fearlessness. What a wonderful gift this is—to have every anxiety under His lordship and control. In fact, God invites us to "approach the throne of grace with confidence" (Heb 4:16). Because Jesus has abolished fear through His redemptive work, we are at liberty to enter into the very presence of God with our heads held high.

Perhaps you are like me, and feel very intimidated about being in the presence of impressive people. Occasionally, I have the privilege to meet with some pretty famous men and women, and I always get very nervous. I'm afraid that I will say or do something stupid.

I recall one particular time when Kimberly and I were traveling to visit my parents. We were in Virginia, where heavy snowfall is uncommon, and so when they occasionally have a snowstorm everything shuts down completely. We were within a hundred miles of my parents' home when the roads closed off and we were forced to stop and to get a room in a tiny hotel. This hotel was small. In fact, there was only one phone, and when I went to use it, I was flabbergasted to find myself in line behind Chuck Colson.

As you probably know, Mr. Colson had a prominent role in the Nixon administration's Watergate scandal in the 1970s and later wrote a wonderful book titled *Born Again* that tells how his life was transformed when he accepted Jesus Christ in a prison cell while serving time for his part in the Watergate affair. After his release, he began to reach out to help other prisoners find the power of Jesus, and his efforts grew into a powerful, fruitful ministry called Prison Fellowship.

There I was, behind Chuck Colson, a man I deeply admire. I stepped back to a polite distance, but I could hear his conversation about an upcoming primary election. As it turned out, it was a discussion that would go on and on. I tried my best to act patient and nonchalant, as though I didn't even know who he was. And then along came my wife, Kimberly.

"Glenn, you've got to get on the phone now and call your parents. Every minute of delay will cause them to worry more," Kimberly said as she urged me to tap Mr. Colson politely on the shoulder and let him know we needed the phone.

"But, honey," I whispered, "that's Chuck Colson on the phone."

Kimberly was undaunted, insisting that I interrupt him. And she was right. I'm pretty sure that Chuck Colson would have graciously let me use the phone to call my parents—if I had not been afraid to talk to him. The point I am making is that Jesus has freed us to approach God—a Person who is far more impressive than any celebrity. We are free to "tap Him on the shoulder" any time we have an urgent need, and we don't need to stumble or stammer in embarrassment.

What a friend we have in Jesus—a friend who wants to introduce us to His Father and help us get acquainted without fear or intimidation. In and of ourselves, we have every reason to fear God and to cower before Him in shame and embarrassment. But when we choose to accept the friendship of Jesus, God puts aside all the things we have to be ashamed of and we can stand before Him fearless, because we have Jesus standing with us—our perfect Advocate and Friend. He takes us home to meet His Father. And even though we still stand in awe of Him, we no longer need to cringe in fear, because in effect He says, "My Son's friends are always welcome in my house."

Getting Up Close and Personal

What is your greatest fear? Are you most afraid of death or illness? Is fear of failure the phantom that chases you through your dreams? Are you so attached to another person—a spouse or a child—that you are terrified of losing them?

Do you have a secret that follows you everywhere you go? Maybe you are afraid of losing credibility with your boss or respect from your family and friends.

Fear of earthquakes, tornadoes, hurricanes—how high are natural disasters on your list of things to be afraid of?

Are you so driven to earn money because you are afraid of not having enough that you miss the pleasure of the simple things in life? Everyone is afraid of something, but you don't have to carry around your fear for even one more torturous minute.

Remember that "God did not give us a spirit of timidity, but a spirit of power, of love, and of self-discipline" (2 Tim 1:7). Of course, until God takes us to Heaven, Satan is forever going to try his best to convince us that we do, indeed, need to be afraid. He will study us and root out our areas of weakness.

For example, I will never completely shake my reluctance to be in the presence of famous people, and I'm certainly not going to go shopping for a pet snake. But when Satan taunts us, we can remind him of Timothy's verse and of many others that testify to the power of God's Spirit Who indwells us. And when we draw upon Him, our enemy the devil cowers in terror.

All Is Well

A story is told about a young American pilot during World War II who was on a mission when he encountered an enemy plane.

The Japanese bomber seemed to fall from the sun, diving at more than four hundred miles per hour. Machine gun bullets ripped first through the wing and then the fuselage of the young man's plane. With the swift reflexes of a nineteen-year-old, he flipped his plane into a barrel roll and dove, then whipped up into a loop in an attempt to get behind his adversary.

It was to no avail. He was dealing with an experienced Japanese pilot, and the sparring continued until the enemy pilot was able to get the American in his sights. Bullets shattered the plane, smoke billowed from the engine, and the aircraft spiraled down into the jungle below. With a tremendous blow, the plane crashed. The courageous young man was barely alive, but he managed to stagger from the wreckage and drag himself to a safe distance in case the plane exploded. There he was, alone in the jungle of a deserted island, wounded and dying, far away from his family and the sweetheart waiting for him in the States.

This is a nightmare we all fear—spending our last moments of life in pain and loneliness. It seems a tragic waste. But when the young pilot's body was recovered, a crumpled piece of paper was found clutched tightly in his hand. On it were scrawled the words of an inspiring hymn, "It is well, it is well with my soul."

For this young man, death had been swallowed up in victory. Even today, his story is a moving testimony of human triumph in the face of death—because this man had placed his trust in Jesus Christ.

Is it well with your soul? Have you taken the antidote for fear that is offered by the Fearless One?

If not, Jesus is waiting to offer you the spiritual elixir that will free you from the crippling terrors that rob you of the peace known to the young American pilot.

The only action required of you is one decisive moment of trust.

Applying the Antidote

An excellent exercise for coping with fear is to keep a "fear list." Simply keep a little notebook handy and every time you feel anxious or fearful about anything, jot it down. Be sure to note the date and time.

Periodically, read through your journal and note how many of your fears actually came to pass—and how many did not. You'll be surprised at all the concerns you had that proved to be ungrounded and, with practice, you can actually learn to put your fears aside.

For: Fear

"When I am afraid, I will put my trust in You."

—Ps 56:3 (NASB)

Chapter 13

Toxic Expectations

℞

I don't know the secret to success, but the key to failure is to try to please everyone.

—Bill Cosby

℞

HE WAS ONLY THIRTY years old, yet He was entrusted with the most important project in all of human history. He had only three years to accomplish His mission with no pay, no benefits, and no perks. There were no professional titles preceding his name—no advanced, specialized degrees that gave him social credibility.

His name was Jesus Christ, and what was expected of Him was humanly impossible. But He met the deadline and accomplished His assignment—right down to the last detail.

As I've studied the life of Jesus Christ, I've been impressed not only with what He accomplished through His work, but also with His working style. Jesus assumed the most overwhelming responsibility ever delegated to any human being, yet scripture characterizes Him as a man who was balanced and who knew how to pace Himself.

And while it is true that Jesus was divine, He was also fully human. His body had the physical limitations we battle. He got tired, sick, and hungry, and He was not exempt from stressful pressures. He was, however, an expert at handling them, and one of His reasons for dwelling here was to be a living example of how to manage our own lives so that we can successfully accomplish the work God gives us to do.

Most of us conduct ourselves in a very different way than Jesus did. We take on too much, move too fast, and place unreasonable demands on ourselves. "Success" is one of our highest values, and we have challenging ways of evaluating what that means. In short, we impose expectations on ourselves—expectations we are not capable of living up to. We set ourselves up to fail, and then we beat ourselves up for not succeeding.

In our society, we admire people who take on the world. Parents tell their kids to "shoot for the stars." "You can do anything you want if you set your mind on it and are willing to work hard," we're taught. From early childhood on, we are conditioned to expect the best from ourselves. But there is a fine line of difference between expecting "the best" and expecting "too much." We need to beware of crossing that line, because when we do our expectations become toxic.

How can we protect ourselves from "toxic expectations"? By looking at the way Jesus lived His life. And since He sacrificed His rightful place in Heaven to show us how to live, we owe Him the courtesy of studying His example and applying it to our lives.

With that in mind, let's look at seven "Christlife" principles for managing expectations that He modeled while He lived on Earth.

Christlife Principle #1: Identification

High expectations are not necessarily bad. It can be motivating when we are challenged by our own personal goals, or even by the gifts and callings that others see in us. It's good to strive for the best we have within us, but when our own expectations or those of others begin to drive us compulsively and cause us to be overwhelmed with pressure, those expectations can become like an idol in our lives. They take over, control us, and become the focus of all we do. They poison our relationships with other people and, more importantly, with God.

Believe me, as a pastor I struggle with this every single day, as I'm sure you do. If you are in the practice of keeping your schedule written down in a planner, just go back and glance at all the events, responsibilities, appointments, and commitments you tried to juggle last month. Does it make you tired?

It makes me tired to review my schedule. Yet, I have to say, "Well, everything on the agenda was important. It was all 'God's work.'"

But was it?

Did God intend for me to take on this much or is it sort of a spiritual disguise for personal, impossible expectations I load on myself? Jesus said that His yoke is easy, and the burden he places on us is light (Matt 11:30). I don't believe He calls us to bite off more than we can chew. After all, we are limited physically and we cannot expect the quality of our efforts to match the quantity of our expectations when they are as numerous as those described in the above profile.

Too often we're driven more by our own compulsions than by God's chosen directives. And if we are truly honest, the root of this lies in our own desire to be recognized as somebody who can do it all.

As Christians, we should instead desire that our activities bring recognition and glory to Jesus. So the first thing we can do to deal with toxic expectations is to examine our motives—to look at ourselves honestly and assess whether the agenda we follow is truly God's agenda or one we have embraced for our own, self-focused reasons.

We see this principle in a statement Jesus once made: "Even if I testify on my own behalf, my testimony is valid, for I know where I came from and where I am going" (John 8:14). Jesus knew who He was, and what He was supposed to do, and He did not allow the expectations of people around Him to confuse Him or to break His concentration. We need to follow His example.

In the 1960s, people became obsessed with the notion of "finding yourself." Some even used it as a reason to abandon their responsibilities in a quest for self. I'm not suggesting that we follow this example. However, it is true that when we don't have a grip on who we are, we are more vulnerable to the pressure of others to try to be somebody else.

Jesus faced this kind of pressure from people around Him who had their own idea of what His agenda should be. Some envisioned Him as a political leader of Israel. Others wanted Him to be a military genius—to throw off the yoke of Rome and become a worldwide leader. But Jesus knew that God's plan went beyond the political or military objectives of individuals. He was attuned to His Father in Heaven and submissive to the plan that would lead temporarily to a torturous Cross rather than a powerful throne. He also knew what would happen after the Cross and how much better that agenda was for Him—and for all humanity.

A lot of the stress we endure comes from our attempt to be someone we are not designed by God to be. We may think we want His will in our lives, but in reality we are far more affected and directed by the will of other people or ourselves. So we become distracted from God's purpose. Jesus refused to be distracted. I think of the biblical phrase that describes how He "set His face toward Jerusalem" (Luke 9:51). He knew and accepted God's agenda and kept His eye on the finish line, and as Christians we, too, should focus on finishing our race.

Christlife Principle #2: Dedication

Jesus once said, "By myself I can do nothing. I judge only as I hear and my judgment is just. For I seek not to please myself, but Him who sent me" (John 5:30).

Jesus knew who He was. He also knew Who He was working for. It wasn't Mary or Joseph. It wasn't the twelve friends who supported

Him in ministry. It wasn't the Roman emperor. He was doing God's work, and it was God He was interested in pleasing.

It goes without saying that we can't please everyone, yet we still seem to try. And the more people we try to please, the more we are spread thin to the point that we can't really please anybody.

When I was a kid, I loved to read Aesop's Fables, so a few years ago I bought a copy of this classic for our children. If you are familiar with these stories, you know they are short tales with a moral lesson. Let me share one:

A father and son were going to the marketplace with their donkey when they came upon a group of people who ridiculed them because they were both walking when one of them could have been riding on the donkey. So the man got on the donkey and his son walked alongside. Shortly they came upon a second group of people who said, "Isn't that terrible for that man to ride the donkey and make his son walk?"

They switched places and continued on their way until they came upon a third group of people who were outraged that a young man was riding while the older man walked. Both men climbed onto the donkey's back and proceeded until they met the local animal rights group. "How outrageous that those two big men are both riding on a poor donkey!" they chided.

Finally, the man and his son arrived at the marketplace, carrying the poor donkey, who was tied to a pole—and looking very foolish indeed.

Like the father and son in this fable, we also end up looking foolish and being ineffective when we listen to everyone and try to do what they expect of us. Jesus focused on pleasing just one Person—His Heavenly Father—and we will simplify our lives if we follow suit.

Christlife Principle #3: Organization

It is not always possible to simplify our lives. Even when we have our priorities in order and our commitments under control, we can still be overwhelmed by pressures and expectations. The expression "the tyranny of the urgent" is an apt description of life in modern society. We cannot always control what is expected of us, but we can manage our lives better if we are organized.

The first step is to prioritize, and specifically to seek God's guidance regarding His priorities, rather than our own. Often I find myself spinning my wheels, and I have a tendency to blame my stress on other people.

One time, I felt like I was going to explode from the pressure and so I began to pray. As I did, God convicted me that I was not being honest with myself. It was almost as if He were saying, "Why don't you come clean and say it like it is? You blame your stress on other people, but it's really your choice to be in this state. You are not in a 'have to' situation. You are in a 'choose to' situation."

As I thought about this, I realized that we impose a great deal of stress on ourselves because we choose to. There are times, of course, when we don't have a choice. Certainly there are occasions when we have work projects that we must complete in order to hold on to our jobs, and there are situations in our families that arise that demand our immediate and complete attention. But probably more than half the stress we wrestle with comes from tasks we've taken on by choice. When we do this, we are yielding to our own inner compulsions—not God's divine calling—and setting ourselves up for eventual burnout.

If we let the Holy Spirit direct and control our actions, then we will never become overloaded to the point that we burn out. I once read about a bridge that had a ten-ton limit. For nearly fifty years, this bridge held up as literally millions of trucks carrying tons of cargo rolled over it. Then one day a trucker had a load of logs that exceeded the ten tons in weight, and he ignored the limit. The bridge collapsed under the truck. We are a lot like that bridge. We can hold up for a long time and bear a lot of heavy loads if we respect our limitations. And the best way to be in touch with those limitations is to cultivate a close relationship to God and to be open to His leading.

Christlife Principle #4: Delegation

One of the first steps we need to take is to admit that we can't do it all. In His earthly ministry, Jesus set the precedence by delegating responsibility to His disciples. Scripture reports that:

> *Jesus went up on a mountainside and called to Him those He wanted, and they came to Him. He appointed twelve—designating them apostles—that they might be with Him and that He might send them out to preach and to have authority to drive out demons. (Mark 3:13–15)*

Sometimes we get the notion that we have to save the world on our own, but Jesus chose to make it a team effort. He showed us that it's appropriate to ask other people to share the burden of our responsibilities. After all, two is better than one, and great things happen when people work together to accomplish a task for the Lord.

Rick Warren writes this about toxic expectations:

> *Do you know why we get uptight and tense? Because we think that everything depends on us. Here I am, Atlas, holding up the cares of the world—they're all on my shoulders. If I happen to let go, the world will fall apart. But when I really do let go, the world doesn't fall apart.[1]*

Have you ever had an experience like this? You thought you had to personally take care of something in order to ensure that it was done right, but when you were forced to ask someone to help you, you discovered that the world didn't end. In fact, the two of you did a much better job together than you could ever do by yourself. That's why many management experts recommend you delegate a task when someone can do it 80 percent as well as you can do it yourself. This is a "win-win" situation. Your helpers get the satisfaction of expanding their skills, and you get more time to devote to higher-priority items.

Since delegation is obviously wise, why don't we practice this principle more often? There are two reasons. First, some of us are perfectionists. We think a task has to be done perfectly, according to a standard to which only we can attain. When you think of it, this perfectionist standard is really a way of saying, "I'm the best." It's a cover-up for egotism. In reality, isn't it at least possible that someone else could also have the capability to do a good job? And isn't it erroneous to think that if we try to do it all, we can hit that perfect standard? We are limited by our human capacities, and if we are spread too thin, we will ultimately sacrifice quality in our performance—and in the relationships that will suffer because we have no time to nurture them.

A second reason we don't delegate responsibility to others is quite the opposite of perfectionism. Some of us are afraid to share a task with another person because we fear they will do it better. Again, ego drives our motives. If we are secure in our relationship with God, we must acknowledge that God has work for all of us to do. We don't need to feel threatened when He provides someone to help us. There's enough work to go around, and we might be getting in God's way of using another person to do something He wants them—not us—to do.

Christlife Principle #5: Meditation

We've looked at four principles to help us get our expectations under control, but how do we actually ensure that we practice those principles? As human beings, there is a tendency to "do it my way" rather than God's way. It's very hard work to stay on track, but we can help ourselves by spending time with Him every day. We need to have frequent two-way conversations—pouring out our heart through prayer, then listening to Him as we meditate on His Word. The more we practice this spiritual discipline, the more we will be attuned to His priorities.

Again, we see that Jesus modeled this principle for us during His life on Earth. Mark tells us that Jesus rose early in the morning, before the light of dawn, and stole away to a solitary place to pray (Mark 1:35). For many people, this is the best time of day to meet with God. After a good night's sleep and before we get on the fast track, our minds and bodies are fresh. What better time to meet with the Master to commit our hands, our hearts, and all our energy to His use.

Morning is a good time—but not the only time—to have a standing appointment with the Lord. Find the time that works best for you. I've found it very helpful to use the time I spend commuting to and from work as a time to talk to God. Of course, it's important to remain alert and to pay attention when you are driving, but look around you the next time you're on the road. How many people do you see talking on cellular phones? Wouldn't it be better to turn off the phone, radio, or CD player and "call God" instead?

Morning time, commute time, lunchtime, evening time. It doesn't matter so much when you spend time with God as it does that you do it every day so that you are growing closer to Him all the time. As you draw near to Him and abide in Him, you will begin to be more like Him and it will be easier to discern His will for you.

Christlife Principle #6: Recreation

Just as we need to make daily time with God a high priority, we also need to make time for personal rest and recreation. In addition to making time for worship, God commanded us to rest on the seventh day because He understood our tendency to burn ourselves out with activity. When we obey His "sabbath principle," we function according to His plan and design. But when we ignore it, we become frazzled and exhausted.

The Bible tells us that Jesus practiced this in His own life. With the masses coming to Him, He barely had time to eat. Yet He regularly called His disciples aside to a quiet place to rest because He understood that our physical bodies function best when they are rested (Mark 6:31).

Christlife Principle #7: Transformation

There is one more Christlife principle to help in our struggles with toxic expectations, and that is to practice surrendering them all to Jesus. When we do, He transforms us. He beckons us to come to Him when we are weary, and He promises to replace those conditions with peace and calm. "My yoke is easy, and my burden is light," He assures us, also promising to give our bodies and souls the refreshing rest they need (Matt 11:28).

A poetic meditation based on the Twenty-third Psalm paints a serene picture of how Jesus transforms our minds and bodies:

The Lord is my pace-setter, I shall not rush. He makes me stop and rest for quiet intervals. He provides me with images of stillness, which restores my serenity. He leads me in ways of efficiency, through calmness of mind, and His guidance is peace. Even though I have a great many things to accomplish each day, I will not fret, for His presence is here. His timelessness, His all importance will keep me in balance. He prepares refreshments and renewal in the midst of my activity by anointing my mind with His oils of tranquility. My cup of joyous energy overflows. Surely harmony and effectiveness shall be fruits of my hours. For I shall walk in the pace of my Lord and dwell in His house forever.[2]

Are you enjoying a life defined by stillness, serenity, balance—His oils of tranquility? No matter how busy you are, Jesus wants to be your pacesetter. So if you are heavy-laden with burdens and expectations, come to Him now. He is waiting to give you rest.

Applying the Antidote

Jesus may be your Savior, but is He also the Lord of your schedule? Here's a good spiritual habit to practice on the first day of every week. Why not make this a regular part of your quiet time with God?

1. Sit down alone with your appointment book and look carefully at the week ahead of you.

2. Use a colored highlighter to mark each activity scheduled into your upcoming week.

3. Go back and think about each appointment and activity, asking yourself, "Is this part of God's agenda or my agenda?"

4. As He leads you, delete scheduled items that can be eliminated. Add others that He might bring to mind. Then commit your schedule to Him.

5. And have a great week!

For: Unrealistic Expectations

"Speaking the truth in love, we will in all things grow up into him who is the Head, that is, Christ."

—EPH 4:15 (NIV)

Chapter 14

The Ultimate Antidote

୶

*I have come that they
may have life, and have
it to the full.*

—JOHN 10:10 (NIV)

୶

IN PREVIOUS CHAPTERS, I have tried to offer Christian readers some practical, powerful, and relevant biblical helps in dealing with life's most deadly emotional and spiritual toxins. I sincerely hope and pray that you have found the contents practical and inspiring, and that by applying the antidotes for life's toxins, you will enjoy the rich, full life Jesus came to give you.

This closing section is meant for those of you who are still in a state of spiritual death. Do you know that we are all born in a condition of original sin, and that sin is the spiritual toxin that takes away your right to life. Forever.

But there is an antidote that will reconcile you to God and restore that life. Forever!

If you have never received Jesus Christ as your Lord and Savior, I encourage you to do so right now by taking the following, simple steps:

1. Admit your condition before God: "For all have sinned and fall short of the glory of God" (Rom 3:23).

2. Recognize Jesus Christ as God's only solution to your condition: "Jesus answered, 'I am the way and the truth and the life. No one comes to the Father except through me'" (John 14:6).

3. Receive Jesus Christ as your Savior and Lord: "Yet to all who receive Him, to those who believe in His name, He gave the right to become children of God" (John 1:12).

4. Say a prayer, asking Jesus to cleanse toxic sin from your life, once and for all. Pray along the following lines:

> *Dear Lord Jesus, I know that I am a sinner and need Your forgiveness. I believe that You died for my sins. I now receive You into my heart and give You the control of my life. I want to trust You as Savior and follow You as Lord.*

After you have received Christ as your Savior, I encourage you to be baptized out of obedience to His command: "Go and make disciples ... baptizing them in the name of the Father and of the Son and of the Holy Spirit" (Matt 28:19).

May God bless you and lead you in living a "toxin-free" life.

Notes

Chapter Two: Toxic Stress

1. Barbara Bush, commencement address at Wellesley College, Wellesley, Massachusetts, June 1, 1990. See text online at http://bushlibrary.tamu.edu/biographies/firstlady/wellesleyspeech.html.

2. David R. Mains, *Eight Survival Skills for Changing Times* (Wheaton, Ill.: Victor, 1992), 33.

Chapter Eight: Toxic Worry

1. Dale Carnegie, *How to Stop Worrying and Start Living* (New York: Simon & Schuster, 1948), 2.

Chapter Nine: Toxic Resentment

1. Keith Korstjens, *Not a Sometimes Love* (Waco, Tex.: Word, 1981), 13–14.

2. This anonymous piece has circulated extensively in print and on the Internet.

Chapter Ten: Toxic Temptation

1. C. S. Lewis, *The Screwtape Letters and Screwtape Proposes a Toast* (New York: MacMillan, 1973), 53–54.

Chapter Eleven: Toxic Depression

1. Clyde M. Narramore, *How to Handle Feelings of Depression* (Grand Rapids, Mich.: Zondervan, 1969), 11–12.

Chapter Twelve: Toxic Fear

1. "The Rekindling of Hell," *U.S. News & World Report,* March 25, 1991.

Chapter Thirteen: Toxic Expectations

1. Richard Warren, *Answers to Life's Difficult Questions* (Wheaton, Ill.: Victor, 1985), 16.

2. This meditation has circulated widely on the Internet and is variously attributed.